PAUL ALLEN

YOUR ETHICAL BUSINESS

How to plan, start and succeed
in a company with a conscience

D0414131

PAUL ALLEN

YOUR ETHICAL BUSINESS

How to plan, start and succeed
in a company with a conscience

Published by

n g o . m e d i a

Sponsored by

Your Ethical Business: How to plan, start and succeed in a company with a conscience
First published in the UK in 2007 by ngo.media ltd
Unit 4, 25a Vyner Street,
London E2 9DG, United Kingdom
www.ngomedia.org.uk

Editor: Gideon Burrows

Consultant editors: Charlie O'Malley, Heather Wilkinson

Design and layout: Glock Design

Printed on recycled paper by Scotprint, Haddington

A catalogue record for this book is available from the British Library.

ISBN 10: 0955369509
ISBN 13: 9780955369506

CONTENTS

About the author

Paul Allen is a freelance writer and author. His work has appeared in The Times, The Guardian, New Internationalist and Social Enterprise magazine, among other publications.

Paul read modern languages and business studies at the University of Wales in Swansea. He worked as a translator before moving into journalism. Today, he lives and works in east London, where he writes about social, ethical and environmental issues for the national and international press.

Acknowledgements

This book could not have been written without the help and support of a number of people. I would like to extend a special thank you to Gideon Burrows at ngo.media for his vision, commitment and unwavering belief in the project. I hope this is the kind of book you would have wanted to read when you started out.

A massive thank you also to all the inspirational entrepreneurs who generously shared their advice and experiences of their ethical businesses. I am especially grateful to: Charlie O'Malley at P3 Capital; Heather Wilkinson at Striding Out; Bates Wells & Braithwaite for their assistance with Chapter 8; Elaine James and Giulia Kapp at Koan; Richard Reed at Innocent Drinks; Tim West at Society Media; William Ferguson and David Lamb at Triodos Bank; and Uday Thakkar at Red Ochre.

I would also like to thank Carsten Glock and Hanna Sundén at Glock design, Caspar van Vark, Jane McDonald, Trina Wallace at ngo.media, and Vicki Arnold at Starfish PR, for their excellent work on the book.

Finally, a huge thank you to my parents for all their support, and to Anna for living through every chapter.

Foreword

Charlie O'Malley, co-founder, P3 Capital

IF YOU'VE PICKED up this book then you're probably either thinking of starting an ethical business or you're running one already. You're in good company.

Apart from famous ethical business names like Anita Roddick, Jamie Oliver and Richard Reed, there are thousands of others who are also building exciting, dynamic and often high-growth ethical enterprises. And they're doing it in all sectors of the economy: from manufacturing to retail, banking to telecoms, advertising, catering, forestry, venture capital, energy, publishing, insurance, construction, law, and more.

The entrepreneurs behind these businesses believe passionately in their causes: reducing environmental destruction; providing a living wage for workers in developing countries; ensuring animals are treated compassionately; creating inspiring places to work; producing natural products without harmful chemicals; providing work for the long-term unemployed; developing ethical investment opportunities.

If you're reading this book then you probably already know what you are passionate about. You'll have a sense of what matters to you, and how you want to do things differently. If you can combine this with commercial acumen, you'll already have two of the key ingredients for creating a successful ethical business.

Starting and running your ethical enterprise won't be a walk in the park. As well as all the normal challenges of running an early-stage business, you'll also have social and environmental considerations to address. As a pioneer of a new way of doing business, you'll come up against both resistance and inertia. Behind you may be the security of a salaried job, in front the challenge of building something from scratch. You'll need total dedication and have to dig deeper than ever before.

But if you're successful in overcoming the challenges of the early years, your purpose beyond profit will provide deep foundations for a business built to last. If you do it right, you won't be addressing social and environmental issues "in addition", you'll have them woven into the essence of your business – what we call at P3 Capital "business the way it ought to be".

For most of the entrepreneurs we come across in this sector, their core values are non-negotiable. That's the starting point. The task then is finding customers who will pay more for your product or service than it costs to deliver it to them and all that is required to make that happen: building your team, identifying suppliers, finding investment, developing your infrastructure, creating your brand, getting your sales strategy right, nurturing customer relationships, and more.

At P3 Capital we're surrounded by inspirational, passionate and committed ethical entrepreneurs. Sometimes, it can feel as if the whole world thinks like we do. It doesn't.

But running an ethical business shouldn't be anything special. At the end of the day, it is about good business. Businesses have always been about meeting human needs – an ethical business is simply one that thinks deeply about what those needs really are and thinks creatively about how those needs can be met without damaging other people or the environment.

Given that there are 1,001 things to think about when starting up any business, let alone one that cares about its social and environmental impact, Paul Allen has done a great service in providing this how-to handbook as a guide through the questions and challenges you'll face.

Your Ethical Business won't answer every question you have, because no two ethical businesses are alike. But having a copy of this book to hand will make your task a whole lot easier. It will inspire you to think more thoroughly about your ethical enterprise, ensure you don't overlook critical issues, and will increase your chances of success.

In supporting this book, our sincere hope is that a whole new cohort of entrepreneurs will be inspired to start and grow successful businesses that adhere to the philosophy set out in these pages.

One day, we believe that what currently seems remarkable in ethical enterprises will just be normal business. For the sake of our planet and our society, may that day be soon.

P3 Capital is a consultancy firm that provides a range of strategic advisory services to dynamic, high-growth businesses whose products and services create social and environmental value.

www.p3capital.com

Introduction

FLICK THROUGH ANY newspaper or magazine and you will probably find a green supplement or "ethical living" column. As a nation, we have never been so interested in social and environmental issues, and it's not hard to understand why.

Global warming is the single biggest threat to our planet. Climate scientists warn that unless we stop the rise in the world's surface temperature, we will soon be facing an environmental catastrophe. The UK government wants a 20 per cent cut in carbon dioxide emissions by 2010. But levels have been increasing, not falling, in recent years. Deforestation. Unclean technologies. Pollution. We know what has to change – and it's not just the planet we are worried about either. Despite years of promises by world leaders, trade between rich and poor countries continues to be stacked in the wealthier nations' favour. For all the talk about ending poverty, the gap between the poorest and richest in society keeps getting wider.

This book is about how small business can make a positive difference. If you are thinking about setting up a company, or are spending every waking hour trying to make a young business succeed, you may feel it's a bit much to expect you to save the world as well. But doing business ethically doesn't require superhuman powers or divine virtue. Ask some of the country's most inspirational ethical entrepreneurs for their motivation, and they will usually shrug and say: "It's just the way we should be doing business."

This attitude is fast becoming mainstream. Ethical business is not about stereotypical, sandal-wearing do-gooders. Nor is it just about fair trade coffee beans. Whether you're an engineer, a farmer, a florist or a web developer, there are hundreds of practical steps you can take to make your business more community spirited and sustainable.

As with every kind of enterprise, ethical business is about giving and taking. Successful, socially responsible companies like The Body Shop have shown that principles and profits are compatible; and while charity will always have its place, often the best way to effect change – as the people at The Big Issue will tell you – is by giving hand-ups not handouts.

Nowhere is this trend being supported more than on the high street. As consumers increasingly shop with their heads and their hearts, so they are seeking out companies that give them more than just a good product. Just look at the stellar rise of ethical brands like Innocent Drinks and Cafédirect. These companies are market leaders, not niche traders.

How did they do it? While scores of books have been written about being better businesses, these are invariably aimed at vast corporations. Indeed, "Corporate Social Responsibility" has become a multi million-pound industry. But given that 99 per cent of all businesses in the UK are small businesses, it is odd that the little people are almost always ignored; especially since from their ranks will emerge the big businesses of tomorrow.

It is true that many smaller companies are already deeply rooted in their local communities. And yet, according to the UK Environment Agency, they also generate about 60 per cent of commercial waste and are responsible for as much as 80 per cent of pollution.

These statistics alone are a good motivation to ensure your business's negative social and environmental footprint is as light as possible from the very start. But perhaps you'll have other reasons too. I have thought of dozens of ways to explain why ethical business is simply the right thing to do, but have never bettered the one given by Clare and David Hieatt, founders of organic fashion brand Howies:

"Every product we make has to pass the 'rocking chair test'. This is something we use to guide us along the path we are taking. So when we are old and grey and sitting in our rocking chairs, we can look back on the company we created with a smile. That's why we go to the trouble of using the best quality materials to make sure our clothing lasts longer. The longer our products last the less impact they will have on the environment, and the bigger our smile will be."

Whatever your idea, I hope this book gives you both the information and inspiration to help you succeed. Your Ethical Business isn't just another start-up book; it won't give you a line-by-line account of how to write "the perfect" business plan (after all, every business is different). Instead, it is a practical, hands-on guide to creating the kind of company that you want to run, packed with real-life stories from the people who have been there and done it. They reckon anyone can do it. So what are you waiting for?

Paul Allen

1 What is Ethical Business?

IN THIS CHAPTER...

- How to find your starting point
- Where your ethics lie
- How to get global results
- Where to draw the line

STARTING A BUSINESS is a golden opportunity to make your mark on the world. But what kind of mark do you want to make? Will your business exist to address a specific issue, or will you be running a "traditional" business along ethical lines? To build your dream company from scratch, you first need to have some idea of what it will look like. That means understanding which values are most important to you and how they could affect your day-to-day decisions.

Being an ethical entrepreneur is all about decisions. Global warming and world poverty might sound like the kind of problems only governments and multinational corporations can solve. But even as a young business, practically every decision you make – from where you source your supplies, to whom you bank with – has the power to influence not just your local community, but the wider world. Indeed, the whole aim of your business might be to tackle a global problem.

Imagine you are thinking of starting an ethical fashion brand. How would you define being "ethical"? Your product might be an obvious place to start. If you intend to use cotton, did you know that cotton agriculture is responsible for a quarter of all global pesticide use? According to the World Health Organisation, pesticides currently cause 20,000 deaths a year through accidental poisonings. For the 400 million farmers in the developing world who work in the cotton industry, these toxic chemicals are an inescapable part of daily life. As well as the immediate effect on their health, fertilisers are also responsible for huge greenhouse gas emissions and the long-term contamination of local water supplies.

As a buyer of cotton for your fashion business, you can do something about this problem. By rejecting conventional producers and sourcing organic cotton (cotton that hasn't been grown or treated with pesticides) you will not only be protecting growers and their families from exposure to poisonous chemicals, but also safeguarding their environment. Because farmers traditionally have to buy their own pesticides, switching to organic could increase their profit margins too.

This is just one example of how a simple business decision – choosing which supplier to trade with – can make a direct, positive impact on other people's lives and their environment. Your business can even help to change the way an industry works. If sufficient companies and consumers demand organic cotton, the global use of pesticides will plummet.

Making a difference

When you consider the grim predictions, it's hardly surprising that global warming is rarely out of the news. Scientists warn that unless we stop the rise in temperature of the earth's surface and oceans, we can expect widespread environmental devastation. Rainforests will die. Sea levels will rise. Droughts and floods will become increasingly commonplace, and most prevalent in countries that are least able to cope with them. On an economic level, the effects of global warming could create the worst global recession in living memory, with many countries facing economic ruin. The government is so alarmed about all these predictions that it has pledged to slash UK emissions of carbon dioxide – the dominant greenhouse gas – and is encouraging other countries to follow suit.

The need for global action is clear, but how does any of that relate to you and your business? One immediate connection is that your business will almost inevitably generate some amount of greenhouse gas of its own. By reducing this, you will already be making a positive contribution.

Local actions *can* produce global results. If you are looking to start a franchise of organic fast food shops, for example, two key ethical decisions will be where to source your ingredients from, and how to transport them.

In 2004, the UK transport sector – principally road traffic – accounted for around 27 per cent of our national carbon dioxide emissions. The use of air freight, meanwhile, which is even more pollutant than road (just 1kg of kiwi fruit flown from New Zealand to Europe discharges 5kg of carbon into the atmosphere), doubled between 1992 and 2002. By supporting local producers and transporting goods in low-emission vehicles you can keep your pollution to a minimum.

You could even go one step further and pay to "offset" any unavoidable carbon emissions. Offsetting is a relatively new concept and not without criticism (see p.56), but the basic idea is simple. You "neutralise" all of your carbon emissions, e.g. electricity and petrol, by paying to plant new trees and supporting energy conservation projects around the world. If you are serious about looking after the planet, these are just a couple of examples of how to reduce your "carbon footprint". We will be looking at many more in subsequent chapters.

What is fair?

In less than a decade, the term "fair trade" has gone from near obscurity to international recognition. For many people, it is now a byword for ethical business. But what does the Fairtrade kitemark really stand for?

The fair trade movement aims to create opportunities for economically disadvantaged producers, usually in the developing world. Traditionally, these growers have had very little power to control what price they receive for their crops on the free market. Fair trade gives growers two main things: a minimum price, which covers the cost of production and amounts to a living wage; and a premium, which is designated for social and economic development in the producing communities. The farmers and workers themselves decide how these funds are to be spent.

Beyond price, fair trade also prohibits child and slave labour, and ensures growers have a safe

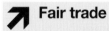

Fair trade

Throughout this book, we use Fairtrade and fair trade in distinct ways. Fairtrade is the specific recognised kitemark awarded to companies that guarantee a fair price to producers for their goods, and contribute in other specific ways to producing communities. The term "fair trade" describes this movement and these principles, of which Fairtrade certification is a part.

workplace, the right to unionise, and an adherence to the United Nations charter of human rights. It also guarantees the protection and conservation of the growers' environment, and promotes long-term business relationships between them and sellers.

Fairtrade Foundation
www.fairtrade.org.uk

Awards and monitors the Fairtrade kitemark in the UK. The Foundation licenses the mark to products that meet internationally recognised standards.

If you want to show that you care about all these things, carrying the Fairtrade kitemark on a product does just that. Currently, only a restricted range of products can carry the mark, but even if your chosen product isn't there yet, there are other ethical badges (see p.199) which may be applicable and can demonstrate that ethical values are central to your business. Alternatively, you can apply the overarching *principles* of fair trade into all your everyday decisions. Whether you are selling a product or a service, this might include how you treat your suppliers, your staff and anyone else that your operations will affect.

With fair trade sales figures up an incredible 265 per cent since 2002, it is clear that consumers have never been more supportive of the *values* represented by fair trade.

Making a contribution

What world issues do you think are relevant to your business idea? You may think it is an advantage if there is an obvious connection. You don't *need* to run a mineral water company, for example, to be concerned that only one quarter of people on the planet have access to clean water, but there will be a clear link between your enterprise and this pressing issue. Doing something about it will not only align your business and ethical goals, but it can also help customers to "get" what your company is all about.

Nevertheless, your company can equally be a means to an end; perhaps to give time, money or other resources to a campaign or cause, which may on the surface have very little in common with your core business. The World Health Organisation (WHO) estimates that 27 million children do not receive basic medical vaccines and 2 million people die of vaccine-preventable diseases every year, predominantly in developing countries. You don't have to sell products for children, or run a medical service, to want to do something about this.

It's not just in the developing world where your business can make a real difference. When professional training consultant Carmel McConnell read that for one in four kids in the UK, the only hot meal they get is at school, she decided to tackle the problem herself. Evidence shows that these malnourished children (who frequently come from economically disadvantaged families) find it very difficult to concentrate and therefore to do well at school. This can damage their career prospects, effectively locking them into a cycle of poverty.

When Carmel heard that many primary school kids in her East London borough of Hackney were coming to school too hungry to learn, she began buying and delivering breakfasts to them before going to work.

The response was so positive that she decided to scale back her consultancy and focus on her Magic Breakfast project. To make it work, however, she needed funding. So in 2002, she started up Magic Outcomes, a company specialising in corporate team-building and leadership training. Magic Breakfast receives 100 per cent of Magic Outcomes' profits. In 2002, Carmel and her team delivered 3,600 breakfasts to local schools. By 2006, this number

Magic Breakfast
www.magicbreakfast.co.uk

Charitable project providing breakfast to UK primary schools, aiming to improve children's ability to concentrate in class. Funded by the profits of Magic Outcomes, a business and education consultancy.

had grown to 100,000.

Despite being one of the richest countries in the world, the UK faces many different social problems: domestic violence, housing shortages, childhood obesity and homelessness are just a few. There are dozens of issues that your new company could help to transform, and Carmel's lesson is that you *can* combine your ethical beliefs with a successful business model.

Unlike Carmel however, you don't have to oversee everything yourself. A less hands-on approach could be to donate a percentage of your revenue or profits to an existing charity which already works in the relevant field.

Alternatively, if the whole point of your business is that it makes a *direct* contribution to a social problem, you can keep things even simpler. If you are passionate about helping people with physical disabilities to find work, for example, you could start up a specialist recruitment company to do just that. You only need to stay in business to make a difference.

Finding your comfort zone

Why do you want to start an ethical business? Some people have a burning passion for environmental or human rights issues. Others simply have a vague notion that their business should be as fair and responsible as possible.

Whatever your motivation, it is incredibly straightforward to integrate your beliefs into the business. You *don't* need to be an activist to make it happen, and nor do you need to be an expert on all the issues. As long as you understand which ethical values are most important to you, which ones cannot be compromised, and where you are willing to bend, it will be easy to steer your business in the right direction.

There may be some dilemmas on the way: when you want to open a bank account, for example, you may find that the best interest rate is not offered by the most ethical bank. Some ethical entrepreneurs would argue that you should always support the bank with the most socially responsible practices (e.g. one that does not invest in the global arms trade). Others would say you should take the best interest rate deal because it will help your business to succeed, maximising the social and environmental benefits your business can deliver.

Only you will know what feels right for your company. Throughout this book, we will be looking at other examples of where you will need to define your own personal comfort zone. By considering this and how these decisions will affect real-life situations, you will be ready to make the right choices to get your ethical business off the ground.

2 A New Consumer

IN THIS CHAPTER...

■ Why act now

■ When ethics make business sense

■ How to lay the right foundations

THERE HAS NEVER been a better time to start an ethical business. While politicians and rock stars make noises about stopping climate change and global poverty, people are increasingly looking to the companies they shop and trade with to actually do something about the problem. Big business has been using words like "good corporate citizen" for years, but these have never been more relevant than today. Enterprises solely concerned with profit are like dinosaurs, and caring about people and planet is no longer a niche pursuit. It's becoming the norm.

If you're a budding entrepreneur, these are very exciting times to develop your business idea. Whether you want to create an innovative solution to a particular social or environmental problem, or to simply build the fairest business possible, there are a myriad ways to make your enterprise ethical from the very start. The good news is that it couldn't be simpler. Unlike multinational corporations, for whom "going green" can be like trying to turn around an oil tanker in the middle of the ocean, you can quickly and easily incorporate these values into the heart of your business. As your enterprise grows, so will the impact of these decisions.

Catching the wave

The demand for ethical goods and services in Britain is at an unprecedented high. From the bedroom to the boardroom, there has been an astonishing boom in ethical spending. Whether through fairly traded cotton or one of the growing number of ethical investment share portfolios, UK consumers are increasingly using purchase power to voice their concerns about a wide range of social and environmental issues.

For socially minded entrepreneurs, this is very encouraging news. Every year, the Co-operative Bank measures levels of ethical consumerism in the UK. Between 1999 and 2004, total spending based on ethical and environmental concerns rocketed from £9.3 billion to £25.8 billion a year. In 2006, sales of ethical goods alone hit over £2 billion, up a massive 62 per cent on 2002.

The story of fair trade is perhaps the best-known example of this success. The Fairtrade mark guarantees better prices, working conditions, local sustainability and fair terms of trade for farmers and workers in the developing world. When it was launched in 1994, only one product had Fairtrade certification. Today, the demand for all things fair trade has never been stronger.

⤴ Fair trade facts

■ There are now more than 1,500 different Fairtrade certified products available in the UK

■ Since 2003, the volume of Fairtrade certified products sold in the UK has grown by 111 per cent

■ Sales of Fairtrade certified coffee and bananas have doubled in the last two years

■ One in five cups of filter coffee drunk in the UK today is supplied from a fairly traded source

■ In 2005, worldwide fair trade sales were up one third on the previous year

■ Between 1998 and 2005, the retail value of products carrying the Fairtrade mark leapt from £16.7 million to £195 million

Just as impressive as these figures is the kind of business now embracing fair trade principles. A movement born of small independent growers has now become so powerful that the UK's biggest companies can no longer afford to ignore it. In October 2005, Nestlé, the world's largest coffee buyer (and one of the planet's most boycotted companies) launched its own fair trade blend of coffee. Despite drawing plenty of accusations of "greenwash" (see p.40), this has undoubtedly brought tangible benefits to a huge number of producers.

In March 2006, high-street retailer Marks & Spencer announced it was to replace all 38 lines in its tea and coffee ranges with fair trade alternatives. By autumn, the retailer announced coffee sales in its food halls had increased by 27 per cent. By the end of the year, it had increased its ethical portfolio by introducing fair trade cotton t-shirts, jeans and babywear into its stores. Today, Marks & Spencer is increasingly trying to pitch itself as one of the most ethical retailers on the high street.

Trading in fair trade goods, however, is only one example of making a positive difference. There are literally hundreds more ways to be ethically minded: from how you treat your staff to where you set up your business, and much more besides.

The Co-operative Bank's Ethical Consumerism Report shows that people in the UK are being increasingly choosy when it comes to investing their money. In 2004, the amount of money invested ethically broke through the £10 billion barrier for the first time.

Strong ethical values also help to explain why the Co-operative Bank turned down nearly £10 million of investment in 2005. This was the amount of business it rejected from unethical businesses, such as arms manufacturers and fur traders. Nevertheless, the bank still made a pre-tax profit of £96.5 million that year – and calculated that more than a third of this figure could be attributed to its ethical policies. In other words, sticking to its principles had actually made good financial sense.

There is a very strong business case for ethical enterprise. In September 2006, Sir Richard Branson announced that his company Virgin was to commit £1.6 billion to tackling climate change. At first, this sounded like just another case of corporate billionaire turns philanthropist. But Branson's decision has nothing to do with charity. Instead, the serial entrepreneur is using all the profits from his Virgin air and rail interests over the next 10 years to finance Virgin Fuels, a new renewable energy business, which aims to develop more environmentally friendly alternatives to oil. With fossil fuels running out fast, it could end up being his most profitable – not to mention ethical – venture yet.

Increasingly, however, the impetus for ethical

business is coming from smaller, innovative companies, and from the CEOs of tomorrow. According to research by Ernst & Young, 89 per cent of recent graduates would not work for a company with a poor ethical record. More than half say they would choose an "ideal job" over a better paid one.

For many people, celebrity chef Jamie Oliver's attempts to help disadvantaged young people train and work as professional chefs at his Fifteen restaurant was their first encounter with a small ethical business. Today, there are four Fifteen restaurants worldwide and the Fifteen Foundation continues to inspire unemployed young people every year. More than anything, Jamie's work at Fifteen and elsewhere proves that individuals can change the world. And no, you don't have to be a TV chef for it to happen. Just ask Dale Vince, founder of green energy company Ecotricity, Penny Newman, chief executive of Cafédirect, or Tim Smit, chief executive of award-winning environmental centre the Eden Project.

The Fifteen Foundation
www.fifteenrestaurant.com

Fifteen is a chain of restaurants established by celebrity chef Jamie Oliver, which as well as serving gourmet food, trains young people from disadvantaged backgrounds to become world-class chefs.

The case for ethical business

Starting up a new business is hard work. Budgets can be tight (sometimes non-existent!), initial returns may be small, and there are often personal savings on the line. Adding ethical considerations can increase this financial squeeze. When you choose not to deal with the cheapest supplier on ethical grounds, for example, you are deliberately increasing your cost base. But although behaving ethically might up your outgoings initially, you can console yourself with more than just the moral high ground. There are several clear business advantages to being ethical too:

Public demand

Companies with strong ethical practices have never been in greater demand. In 2004, the desire to help counter climate change amounted to £3.4 billion of consumer spending, an increase of 21 per cent on the previous year. Just being green won't necessarily have customers queuing around the block, but if you can match (or beat) the competition on price and quality and can show your business has stronger ethical credentials, you're onto a winner.

Transparency

Growing media interest, coupled with the rise of watchdog organisations like Ethical Corporation magazine, mean that companies' ethical practices are being scrutinised like never before. If they slip up, consumers will vote with their wallets, or worse; in 2006, Sussex University became the first campus in the country to ban all Coca-Cola products from its students' union in protest at allegedly unethical corporate practices.

Working culture

Studies show that staff are more honest and loyal to companies that are involved in activities that help to improve society. Not only do ethical businesses get the best out of their staff, they also have great employee retention levels, and often find that the best candidates, with similar values, will actively seek them out for jobs.

Investment

It's hardly surprising that purely profit-driven companies are more prone to scandals than their ethical counterparts. Following several high-profile falls from grace, this has become an increasingly important concern for investors. As public support for socially minded business grows, so investors are looking to broaden their portfolios. Besides offering reduced risk, investing in a more-than-profit company can also enhance their own ethical credentials.

PR

Being ethical is a great marketing tool. With consumers increasingly looking to make the right choices for people and planet, being seen as the "good guys" can be more effective than thousands of pounds of advertising spend. "Morality has finally become fashionable," explains Helen Edwards, brand management consultant and lecturer at London Business School.

Cost

Being green can save you money. Many of the best ways to be a more responsible business, such as energy efficiency and local community engagement, can actually help to bring down your overall outgoings.

Innovation

According to networking organisation Striding Out, four in five business leaders believe that ethical companies are more innovative than their counterparts. New developments in fair trade, sustainable products and cleaner technology are all examples of how ethically minded enterprises have challenged the status quo and created better business practices.

How to be ethical

Ethical businesses come in all shapes and sizes. There is no single model, no one-size-fits-all package – and nor are they a new concept. The modern co-operative movement, for example, which embraces the principles of democracy, equality and fairness for its employees, has its roots in the early 19th century. Before them, the Quakers had been delivering profitable businesses along strong social principles for centuries. And even they weren't the first.

Despite this diversity, there is a common thread running through all of these businesses: to meet ethical goals beyond the pure pursuit of profit. This can take different forms, but the results are invariably similar. Ethically minded companies treat others well, look after their own staff, try not to harm the world we live in and selflessly give something back to society. They are the antithesis of unscrupulous corporate greed.

Ethical business, however, is not about being perfect. No enterprise is flawless, and it is important to realise that this does not make your efforts any less worthwhile. It is sad – and more than a bit ironic – that the companies with the most superficial social responsibility policies are often the ones making the most noise about their "ethical credentials", while genuinely ethically minded companies – ever conscious of how much more they could do to improve – consider themselves all too imperfect.

Running a business ethically is not about

achieving perfection; it's about making a positive difference to the world. This practical approach lies at the heart of many of the world's most inspirational ethical companies.

When smoothie company Innocent Drinks decided on its name, for example, it knew it could only do its best to live up to it. "If you call yourself Innocent, you'd better make damn sure that you are," says director and founder Richard Reed. "But the truth is we are definitely not perfect as a company. We strive to be, but we aren't. Then again, we have never made any bones of the fact that we want to be a profit-making, successful company. The important thing is that we do it in a way that we'd be proud of."

The right mix

When you're starting out, how do you know what ethical approach is right for your business? In all likelihood, you will end up adopting a mix and match of different ideas. But even when you decide on a particular mix, there is nothing to stop you adding more as you go along. Practical experience of your industry and meeting other like-minded companies, for example, will help you discover ever more innovative ways to be a better company. As you grow, you may have greater power to influence the behaviour of others in your supply chain too.

There are three base elements of any ethical business. We'll look at these in detail in the following chapters.

Elements of an ethical business

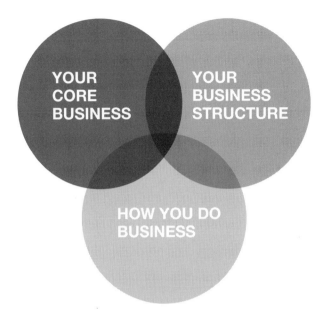

1. Your core business

What you sell reflects the kind of business you are. Some companies are set up specifically to deal with a particular social or environmental problem: recycling companies, fair trade shops, community education providers and green energy suppliers, for example, need only to stay in business to make a positive difference.

Other companies, such as shoe shops, law firms and graphic design agencies, do not combat particular issues. They do still serve a social purpose (by creating jobs and providing useful products and services), but without an obvious ethical core, their biggest challenge is to make sure the way they are run is as fair and green as possible.

What is your core business idea? Are you looking to address a particular issue, or give an ethical twist to a traditional business? Understanding the positive impacts of your new enterprise will help you to understand – and convince others – of its potential.

We will take a closer look at what you sell in Chapter 4: Your Core Business.

2. Your structure

There are many different ways to set up a business. The vast majority of enterprises in the UK are structured as limited companies. But there are several other legal forms, including some new ones designed specifically for ethical business.

The way your business is formed can have a major effect on how it operates. Among other things, the legal structure controls to whom the business is ultimately responsible.

Ben & Jerry's
www.benjerry.com

US-based ice cream company originally founded on social and ethical lines, with a specific ethical mission. Later bought out by Unilever, but run along the same principles.

After seeing their ice cream company, Ben & Jerry's, boom in the 1990s, Ben Cohen and Jerry Greenfield decided to become a public company to fund further growth. The public share issue raised sufficient capital, but after a failed attempt by co-founder Cohen to return the company to private ownership, Ben & Jerry's was bought out in August 2000 by Anglo-Dutch consumer giant Unilever. Greenfield says the multinational offered so much money that, in the end, responsibility to the shareholders won out. Had Ben & Jerry's been structured differently, Cohen and Greenfield may not have been forced to sell the company in the way they eventually did.

The legal structure can also be an integral part of your ethical make-up. Divine Chocolate, for example, which owns the Divine Chocolate brand, is a company limited by shares. As well as receiving fair trade prices, Kuapa Kokoo, the farmers' co-operative that produces the cocoa for Divine, currently owns almost half of the shares in the company. With two places on the board, the farmers' participation in the running of the company also means that producers in Ghana are playing an active role in decisions about how Divine is produced and sold, as well as sharing in the profits.

If you have no idea whether to be a partnership, a company or a co-operative, don't despair. Finding the best legal structure for your business idea doesn't have to be a complicated process. Each different option has its own pros (and cons) and once you measure them against your ambitions for the business, it should quickly become clear which one will be right for you.

We will take a closer look at all the different legal forms in Chapter 8: The Right Structure.

Divine Chocolate
www.divinechocolate.com

UK-based chocolate company, producing the "Divine" brand sold in supermarkets and elsewhere. Guarantees a fair trade price for Ghanaian producers, and also pays a premium to their communities for social projects.

3. How you do business

The final element of the mix is how your business behaves on a day-to-day basis. Often, the way you do business ethically is limited only by your imagination. A law firm, for example, could offer pro bono work to charities, allow its workers flexi-time options, or donate a percentage of its profits to a foundation. An architecture practice could specialise in creating environmentally sound projects, offset its carbon emissions, or use only sustainable products in its designs.

What are the values that you want to run through your business? Deciding which green and socially responsible elements to incorporate will help you to create and refine your ethical business.

We will take a closer look at all these different ideas in Chapter 5: Profit, People and Planet.

3 Food for Thought

IN THIS CHAPTER...

- How to test your idea
- When to take the plunge
- What precautions to take
- How to identify any weaknesses

BEFORE LAUNCHING STRAIGHT into your business, which the remainder of this book aims to show you how to do, it is worth stopping here for a moment. You need to consider some of the biggest issues that businesses which brand themselves as "ethical" are increasingly having to face. It is worth considering them before you start, so you don't get an unpleasant shock later down the line when they can disrupt your business or damage your morale.

Dealing now with the big issues that are bound to come up will help you get ready to enter a competitive marketplace and also prepare you for some of the questions you may come up against along the way.

Testing your idea

Every successful entrepreneur needs self-belief. Many of the best ideas for sustainable businesses have won out precisely because the people who created them refused to believe the doubters and were determined to make them work. When Dale Vince tried to sell the concept of "green energy" in the mid-1990s, he was laughed at by the major electricity suppliers. His company, Ecotricity, is now a multi million-pound turnover business, and those same cynics are falling over themselves to appeal to eco-conscious customers.

If you want to make a positive difference, you may also need a lot of self-confidence to challenge the status quo. But remember that no matter how well intentioned you are, your final business idea must also be able to stand up to criticism.

If you've invented a new kind of technology to channel and use rainwater as "grey" water in the home, for example, an essential stage in your business planning should be to scrutinise your own designs and try to identify any possible faults. Your future customers (and anyone you may ask for finance) will be just as judgmental when they are considering if your idea is any good. Dropping what may ultimately be a bad idea early on will also save you time, effort and money – not to mention unnecessary stress.

When you put your idea to the test, seek as much input from friends and family as possible, but remember that you are looking for honest opinions, not well-intentioned encouragement. Your favourite uncle or grandma is unlikely to be the most objective voice. If you have access to experts in your chosen field of business, they may bring invaluable insights – but remember that their opinions won't always be right, and you may need to exercise caution; if yours is an idea that could be easily copied, be circumspect about whom you tell.

If you are looking to give an existing product an ethical twist, you may have to be careful that another company doesn't steal your idea – and your market – before you've even launched. If your business works, the copycats will follow soon enough.

To test your initial business idea, it's a good idea to use a SWOT analysis: a short document comparing Strengths, Weaknesses, Opportunities and Threats. More than anything, this will give you a chance to see your idea on paper within a broad business context, possibly for the first time. Who are the competition? How does your idea fit into the existing market? If there isn't one, is there really a need for it? These are some of the questions you will need to answer. Many business advice websites, such as Business Balls, have comprehensive SWOT templates, which you can download for free.

Business Balls
www.businessballs.com

Free online resources, forms and tools, for the ethical development of people, businesses and organisations.

Making sure the idea is robust could determine more than just *your* fate. The success or failure of an ethical business can have implications far beyond its owners. If a company which proactively employs disabled people publicly fails, for example, it could put other people off the same idea, and do much more harm than good. While it is unfair to put this kind of responsibility on a single company's shoulders, innovative ethical enterprises may well be judged in this way.

In November 2005, Sheffield Rebuild, which trained "hard-to-reach" unemployed people in construction skills and took on construction contracts, went into liquidation after two major projects were delayed. In its nine years of trading, Sheffield Rebuild had generated turnover in excess of £4 million and given hundreds of unemployed people a first step up into the construction industry. Despite making a real impact on its community, when the company went into voluntary administration it may have wrongly convinced some people that mixing social and financial aims doesn't work.

What to believe?

Being ethical has never been more fashionable. From the most polluting enterprises on the planet to your local café, it seems like every business is trying to present itself as a responsible, ethical company. But what can you really believe?

AccountAbility, a global organisation promoting transparent, socially responsible business practices, says there is a discrepancy between what consumers say and how they behave. According to its 2006 report, What Assures Consumers, 90 per cent of people in the UK oppose caged egg production, but currently only half of eggs sold by major supermarkets are free range.

Similarly, more than 80 per cent of shoppers say they want to reduce food miles, but only a quarter actually look at country of origin labels on the food they buy. The same contradiction applies to services. More than a quarter of UK citizens say they would pay a little more for a green electricity tariff, but only a small minority have actually made the switch.

There is undoubtedly a growing consumer trend towards ethical business. But it seems too that many people are clearly embarrassed about not shopping more ethically – and are actually pretending that they do.

Interestingly, ethical consumerism may also be linked to gender and demographics. According to

AccountAbility
www.accountability21.net

International business membership organisation, which aims to increase businesses' adherence to and professionalism in social and ethical accountability.

a recent survey by research firm TNS Worldpanel Fashion, women appear to be more concerned about ethical fashion than men. Of those who felt ethical production of clothes was important to them, 59 per cent were women and 41 per cent were men.

And while some organic goods are currently priced so high as to put them out of reach for people on low budgets, there were also signs that age affects consumer habits. According to the TNS survey, 58 per cent of people under 25 in Britain don't care how their clothes are produced, almost double the percentage of the more eco-aware over-55 category.

Rachel Neame of ethical clothing company People Tree remains philosophical about the statistics. "If 58 per cent of young people said they don't care, that's 42 per cent who do," she told the Guardian in August 2006. "And that's a very significant number."

Greenwash

Besides dodgy consumer surveys, you might also be concerned about how other companies present themselves. BP, one of the world's biggest oil corporations, currently uses a flower as its logo, and has a habit of describing its business as if it were kick-starting a new green revolution rather than selling polluting fossil fuels. The business watchdog website, Corporate Watch, devotes several pages to unethical practices it says have been carried out by the company. But BP isn't alone in looking to create a deliberately green image. Most of the companies accused of bad business behaviour by Corporate Watch publicly present themselves as a "good corporate citizen".

How could their and other companies' spin affect *your* business? If you are looking to launch a range of locally sourced organic breakfast cereals, you may find that some of your competitors on the supermarket shelf are also promoting themselves as small, all-natural businesses. Never mind that they are flying in non-organic produce from the other side of the world, paying their suppliers a pittance and are actually owned by a multinational conglomerate. If you don't have the marketing budget to set the record straight, it can be frustrating, not to mention financially damaging, to watch ethically minded customers unwittingly make the wrong choice.

Greenwash can affect everything from advertising campaigns and product labelling, to so-called ethical kitemarks, which sometimes aren't actually very ethical at all (see p.199). There is a danger that consumers, faced with conflicting messages and complex decisions, will simply pick the easiest option: i.e. the brands and services they know best. As AccountAbility's research proves, there is a limit to the efforts they may make.

The good news is that you do have many free and highly effective marketing tools at your disposal, such as your product, the internet and even word-of-mouth. We will look at these and many more ways to get your message across later in the book.

When it comes to protecting your business against other companies' greenwash, it helps to have a very clear idea about what makes *your* business ethical. That way, when you speak to journalists, customers, and any other interested parties, you will be best prepared to explain your core values.

Corporate Watch (UK)
www.corporatewatch.org.uk

Web-based magazine and research group keeping a critical eye on the harmful activities of big business, particularly their greenwash.

Timing the leap

★ *Swapping safe, comfortable, but ultimately unsatisfactory employment for the wild world of entrepreneurship could be the biggest decision of your life. But how do you know when it's the right time to take the plunge? Richard Alderson, founder of Career Shifters, gives his top five tips.*

Know yourself

Being clear on what you want out of life and your career is the first step to any successful change. You know you want to start an ethical business, but look carefully at your values and your beliefs. Are they completely aligned with what you want to do?

Talk to others who have done it

Connecting with people who have already travelled the path you want to take is one of the best ways to build the confidence you'll need for what you are about to do. Learn from them, draw inspiration from how they overcame the challenges they faced, and take ideas from their journey that are relevant to yours.

Don't give in to fear

It's natural to feel afraid, but this may be your biggest barrier. Remember that the change you're thinking about may also be challenging for the people around you. Accepting that fear and moving forward will be key to your success.

Consider a staged approach

Jumping straight out of employment into your own business is possible but often not the best route. Consider reducing your hours, going freelance, or taking a sabbatical from your day job. This will give you the breathing space you need to undertake the initial development of your business. It will also make the final leap easier.

Get professional advice

Specialist career change organisations can help your understanding of these issues in a number of ways. Real-life career change success stories and practical exercises can help to build your confidence. Networking sessions with fellow career shifters and experts in your chosen field of business are also great situations to bounce ideas off other people.

www.careershifters.org

Letting go

Are you thinking of starting out on your own? Many of the UK's most successful ethical businesses were created by one inspirational entrepreneur. That person's passion, belief and hard work breathes life into an idea and makes it a reality. In the early days, they will likely be running the show single-handedly: from answering phones to meeting orders and filing accounts.

But as the company grows, it becomes harder to retain this kind of control over the whole business. This should be a good thing, allowing you to focus your energies where they work best. But that can also take a lot of self-discipline.

If you are a passionate cyclist and decide to set up an eco-conscious cycle courier company, you may spend the early days taking care of everything from bike repairs to marketing strategies. If the business expands, you could wind up spending much less time in the bike workshop, and much more in an office – managing orders and client accounts. If this isn't what you want, you will need to think carefully about when and how to bring in other people to take on the aspects that you don't want to run.

A common reason for many business failures is the founder's unwillingness to give up his or her "baby". But often, the person with the energy and spark to get the business off the ground is not the right person to keep it growing. Cafédirect and Howies are just two examples of well-known companies who have brought in experts to take over the day-to-day management of the business.

"Founder syndrome" can manifest itself in a variety of ways. If you have a strong personal connection to your ethics, it can also be easy (but unfair) to assume new people you recruit just won't feel the same way.

Or you might have a fixed idea of where the business is heading, but others might actually identify a much better direction. If you don't listen, you risk running into a dead end.

If you start organising eco-friendly activity weekends for children, you may have a narrow view of your business: a service for children. If the company isn't making enough bookings, you might think about expanding it into a new location, which may present several logistical problems. Someone looking at your company with fresh eyes might identify another simpler solution, such as diversifying into "green" team-building days for companies, which could reinvigorate the business.

Another danger of founder syndrome is that you simply spread yourself too thinly. The best approach is to be ruthlessly honest about your strengths and weaknesses. Where do you most need help? When your business can financially support it, you need to find the best people to fill these gaps.

4 Your Core Business

IN THIS CHAPTER...

- What your business stands for
- How to address ethical issues

WHAT KIND OF business do you want to start? You don't need to sell a particular product or service to make a positive difference, but your core business can affect the kind of ethical impact you can achieve. If you decide to sell fairly traded clothing, for example, a certain level of social and environmental responsibility will run automatically through the heart of your company.

Every one of Cafédirect's boxes of tea and coffee guarantees its global suppliers a living wage. As the UK's largest Fairtrade certified hot drinks company, it has many other ethical policies besides, but its socially responsible core product is the cornerstone of the business. And unlike rival brands, which might devote a small percentage of their product line to fair trade coffee, 100 per cent of Cafédirect's drinks adhere to fair trade principles.

For the vast majority of core products and services however, it's unrealistic to expect this kind of cachet. Arka Funerals in Brighton, for example, provides a very useful service in its local community, but as a business specialising in eco-friendly funerals, it's how the company is run that really makes it ethical (we'll look at this in subsequent chapters).

What is your core business? If you're thinking about setting up a new business, what you sell will often reflect how you are judged. Can you envisage receiving any criticism? Are there any ways to make your central business idea more ethical? When Reed Paget and Marilyn Smith launched mineral water company Belu, they knew that some people were ideologically opposed to the very concept of selling bottled mineral water – an industry which results in huge quantities of plastic being sent to landfill every year. They have tempered the critics by channelling 100 per cent of their profits to clean water projects, and selling their water in fully compostable bottles.

Cafédirect
www.cafedirect.co.uk

The UK's largest fair trade drinks company, which puts over 80 per cent of its profits back into partnership programmes with producers.

Belu
www.belu.org

Bottled water company, which uses bottles made from corn starch and contributes every penny of its profits to water projects in the developing world.

The wrong track

When it comes to a company's core business, there are only a small number of products so inherently harmful that any attempt at social responsibility is meaningless.

Tobacco giant Philip Morris International has long considered itself "a good corporate citizen". Citing the company's policy on using fewer pesticides and its stance against child labour, a company spokesperson argues: "The product can't be the determinant of whether your company is socially responsible. It is whether your behaviour is responsible which is key."

This kind of language might make the CEO sleep better, but it doesn't wash. The World Health

Mondomundi: Trading places

 Guernsey-based food and jewellery retailer Mondomundi has developed three separate strands to its ethical core business.

"We only ever intended to be a fair trade website," explains former accountant Phil Soulsby, who identified a gap in the market for a high-quality, online, fair trade shopping experience. "But since the site launched, we've opened up a shop and also started a trade business, delivering our products to local businesses and restaurants."

Mondomundi only sells products that have the official Fairtrade logo, or are traded through companies listed by the British Association of Fair Trade Suppliers (BAFTS). Its catalogue ranges from tea and coffee, to clothes and art. For Phil, the choice of core product is critical to the business.

"It's not just that everything we buy is accredited," he says.

"While a company like Nestlé might have one fair trade product because they think there's a bit of money in it, I would discriminate against them in favour of (drinks company) Clipper, the majority of whose products are Fairtrade certified because they truly believe in it."

This authenticity has helped Mondomundi build a strong customer base. But such is the widespread availability of fair trade goods in nearby supermarkets, Phil has to compete hard on price and concentrate on growing the business.

"We're looking at opening a second shop," he says. "If you run one shop it's very hard to make good returns. If you have 10, you can afford for the individual returns to be smaller."

If Phil can grow the business to a size where he actually buys beans directly from roasters, he will also be able to cut out the middle levels in his supply chain. This will cut his costs and also help reduce the prices of his fair trade range.

"People should not think it's OK for fair trade to be more expensive," he says. "If we can eliminate unnecessary steps in the chain, we will ensure a higher portion of sales price reaches the producer, and keep shop prices lower.

"That's our main goal: to make fair trade goods accessible to people. The business exists to make a profit, but, much more importantly, we're trying to make a difference."

www.mondomundi.com

Organisation reports that around half the people who smoke die prematurely due to the use of tobacco, and that smoking is currently a greater cause of death and disability than any single disease worldwide. So while reducing pesticide use is a positive gesture, so long as Philip Morris's chief purpose is to get more people smoking, it can never be a good company.

The same criticism can be levelled at weapons makers. Part of BAE Systems' bid to be a socially responsible arms manufacturer is to reduce the amount of chemicals in the paint on the company's guns. "We aim to demonstrate that BAE Systems is both a responsible corporate citizen and a responsible defence company," says the company website. Those on the receiving end of the bullets might disagree.

Companies who use animal testing or fur are often lumped into the same bracket. But while it is easy to make these distinctions, few other areas are so clearly black and white. An oil company's history of corruption, inadequate investment in renewable energy production and mistreatment of indigenous peoples will be clearly deplorable. But anyone who has a petrol-driven car or travels by plane might think twice before denouncing the precious natural resource they also exploit.

Beyond fair trade

Fair trade goods are not the only kind of core business where people and the planet benefit directly from each sale. There are many other intrinsically positive products, such as healthy, nutritious foods made without pesticides, or non-pollutant washing powders. You don't have to stick with existing technologies, either. You could, for example, think about creating an innovative new product that is beneficial for the environment.

Equally, selling goods is only one kind of ethical business. Perhaps your idea is a business approach to solving a specific social problem. Ethical services come in all shapes and sizes. Whether you set up a recycling service, an educational organisation, a medical facility in a developing country or a local community support network, your service can really make a difference.

There can also be fine separating lines between different core businesses. When it comes to energy providers, for example, there are several companies who specialise in selling "green electricity" to UK consumers. But often all they do is buy up existing green energy supply, rather than producing their own. One measure of how committed these companies truly are to renewables is how much they spend per customer on building new sources of green energy. In the WhichGreen 2005 league table, one company, Ecotricity, spent three times more than all the other green suppliers put together. In other words, some ethical core businesses can make a much bigger difference than others.

ScreenReader.net: Breaking down barriers

"Access to the internet is one of the biggest obstacles facing blind and visually impaired people in the UK," says Roger Wilson-Hinds, co-founder of innovative e-commerce company ScreenReader.net.

In 2003, Roger and his wife Margaret, who are both blind, commissioned a specialist software company to help break down this barrier. The resulting "talking software" enables people with little or no sight to write and read letters and emails, fill in forms and surf the web.

Unlike similar software on the market, which is often prohibitively expensive, ScreenReader.net's Thunder technology is designed to benefit everyone because it is free for private home use. With 80 per cent of blind people of working age in the UK currently out of employment, there is a clear need to improve their computer skills and readiness for work.

The Thunder package is free for individuals and can be downloaded from the ScreenReader.net website. The company makes its money by licensing the software to organisations, and by selling other computer aids, such as scanning programmes and high quality synthetic voices, on the web.

"I'm a business person," says Roger, who is currently registering ScreenReader.net as a Community Interest Company (see p.126). "We are a lean, mean e-commerce business – one which will hopefully bring us a long-term income and financially sustain this worthwhile project."

He has already made an impressive start. As well as securing a £10,000 contract with Peterborough Council to make the software available to everyone in the borough, blind and visually impaired people from as far afield as India and Nigeria have been writing to Roger and his team to thank them for making the Thunder software free.

"The talking computer is the gateway to literacy, learning, work and financial independence for blind people," says co-director Margaret. "That's why we were determined to make it accessible to everyone."

www.screenreader.net

5 Profit, People and Planet

IN THIS CHAPTER...

- How to go green
- How to manage your supply chain
- When to put your people first
- How to look after your community

RECYCLING. PROFIT-SHARING WITH employees. Cutting down carbon emissions. Besides your core business, there are countless more ways to put values at the heart of your day-to-day operations.

Whether you want to guarantee fair and open business relationships all the way down your supply chain or simply stock up on fair trade tea in the office kitchen, it's never been easier to give your business an ethical dimension.

Some of these initiatives, such as printing on recycled paper, are easy to implement and will cost you very little. If you plan to donate 10 per cent of your profits to a charitable trust, however, this will have a much more fundamental impact on your finances, and you will need to consider carefully how the business can cope with the extra burden.

But it's not all about weighing up extra costs. Many environmentally sound policies, such as reducing waste, will actually save you money.

JARGON BUSTING... The bottom line

The final line on a company's profit and loss account – the bit that goes on the bottom of the budget – is normally the net income, i.e. profit. As a result "the bottom line" is often used as a euphemism for profit. As an ethical business, you will still take profit making seriously, but you will have other goals too; these are known as extra bottom lines.

A "double bottom line" refers to profit plus a social return: the benefit that society, or a community, gains as a result of your business. The "triple bottom line" includes the environment too. This is best summed up as: Profit, People, Planet.

These extra bottom lines will affect the way you run your business. Your second or third bottom line, for example, might be the reason to make a decision that actually reduces your profits. One example of this is buying more expensive, fairly traded raw materials.

If you manufacture kitchen tables you could insist that all your suppliers are paid a living wage (social return) and that all the wood you use comes from a sustainable source (environmental return).

High-street banks are often accused of failing to look beyond profit when it comes to awarding loan finance. Specialist lenders, such as Triodos Bank and London Rebuilding Society, are often more in tune with the concept of ethical business. But as major corporations increasingly step up their efforts to be ethical, so the awareness of all three bottom lines is growing. Some of these big businesses have even started filing social and environmental audits of their own, along with their regular financial accounts. This is known as "triple bottom line accounting".

In this chapter, we will be introducing a broad spectrum of ethical ideas that you can implement in your business. You may have more suggestions of your own.

Depending on your business idea, you may discover certain industry-specific issues. If you run a construction company, there could be several environmentally friendly options to consider in your choice of raw materials, such as eco-friendly paints, longer-lasting materials and reclaimed wood. Every industry is different; it's a good idea to break down all the different stages involved in your business, and see where your double and triple bottom line could influence your decisions.

In the short-term, you may find you need to put some of your bigger ethical ideas on hold while you grow the business. While these can always be added when the time is right, remember that you should always retain a set of core ethical values that are not to be compromised. If you dilute or abandon those qualities that set you apart from the competition, you could lose your Unique Selling Point (USP). If the whole purpose of your business is to produce natural, chemical-free ice cream, adding flavours and preservatives will completely devalue the ethics that make your business different.

If you do decide to put some grander ideas, such as setting up a charitable foundation, on the back burner to get your business started, the good news is that growth can soon make them a reality. You could even start to dictate how other businesses in your supply chain behave. If your company is successful, you might inspire others in the industry to follow your lead.

Even if you are starting small, however, you will immediately be making a positive contribution. Every single business can incorporate a wide range of ethical ideas into its operations. These positive steps can be divided into four main areas: going green, cleaning your supply chain, putting people first and supporting your community.

Go green

Almost every business has an impact on the environment. Depending on your enterprise, keeping this "footprint" to a minimum could either be a central part of what you sell or simply an over-arching principle as to how you run your everyday business. Companies such as Green Glass, which specialises in turning junk bottles into household glassware, have structured their entire operations around recycling. For them, being green is part of the core business.

But not every company is the same. If you start a car wash business, you could still implement a host of eco-friendly ideas, such as harnessing rainwater and using a green energy supplier.

10 steps to green your business...

1. Save energy

Turning off machines, ensuring buildings are heat efficient and using energy-saving light bulbs are all easy steps to reduce your energy consumption. Switching to a green supplier – ideally one that is investing in new, renewable energies – will also make a difference to your footprint. The Carbon Trust, which specialises in helping businesses go green, reports that the average office wastes £6,000 each year by leaving equipment on

The Carbon Trust
www.carbontrust.co.uk

Free, practical help and advice on saving money by reducing energy use, and to help accelerate innovative low-carbon technologies.

over weekends and bank holidays. Both they and the Energy Saving Trust offer advice on how to integrate energy saving into your daily operations.

2. Offset your carbon emissions

If you run an organic food delivery service, your business may use up a lot of motor fuel and therefore emit a large quantity of carbon dioxide. This harms your ethical credentials. One way of mitigating this is to "offset" your carbon emissions. What this means in practice is paying a specialist company to work out all of your various emissions through heating and travel; then the company redresses the balance by planting woodlands and running renewable energy projects.

Offsetting carbon emissions is now a multi million-pound industry, but it does have many detractors. Despite the industry's assurances to the contrary, the science does seem pretty inexact. Perhaps even more worryingly, many businesses appear to use offsetting to excuse needlessly jetting around the world.

As an ethical business, your greenest option will always be to reduce your emissions as much as possible. Where you ultimately draw the line, however, will be a personal choice. Once you have reached this level, making a contribution to reputable offsetting organisations such as Climate Care will at least make up for some of your remaining carbon footprint.

Climate Care
www.climatecare.org

Commercial 'offsetting' company, which you can pay to account for and offset your carbon emissions by planting trees and supporting environmental projects.

3. Start recycling

Paper makes up approximately 70 per cent of all office waste in the UK. If you want to do something about this, it is easy to set up a recycling scheme in your office – not just for paper, but for metal, glass, print cartridges and other materials too. The website www.recycle-more.co.uk, which lists telephone numbers for every local authority in the UK, will help you put this into practice. Speak to your nearest one to set up collection arrangements.

4. Reduce waste

If you want to start an ethical publishing company, how much paper do you think you will need to use? When printer manufacturer Lexmark carried out a survey of UK offices in 2004, it found that £230 million worth of printed paper is wasted in British businesses every year; incredibly, a fifth of the 110 billion sheets printed (the equivalent of one million trees) are lost on desks, left on the printer or binned within five minutes. If you want to keep your operations waste-efficient, one solution could be to keep the business as electronic as possible.

Cutting down on waste is a challenge for every business. If you want to streamline yours, you could first look at your energy needs. Are you switching off lights, unused plugs and using energy-efficient light bulbs? What about your water usage? Simple steps, such as putting a glass jar in the toilet tank (which reduces the amount of water used per flush) can make a difference. An even more efficient step could be to harvest rainwater to flush your toilets. You can find practical guidance on this and many other waste-saving techniques from the Waste Resource Action Programme.

The best part is that your efforts won't just benefit the environment, but will reduce your energy and stationery bills too. Envirowise, a government-

Waste Resource Action Programme
www.wrap.org.uk

Not-for-profit company which helps businesses to reduce waste, to use more recycled material, and recycle more things more often.

Envirowise
www.envirowise.gov.uk

Offers UK businesses free, independent, confidential advice and support on practical ways to increase profits, minimise waste and reduce environmental impact.

funded agency that advises businesses on how to go green, says that waste typically costs companies 4.5 per cent of their annual turnover. Being more waste aware could save your business a lot of money.

5. Buy green

If you are going to run your business from a building, such as an office or factory, you may need to buy in a lot of supplies: stationery, cleaning products, furniture, toilet paper and hot drinks. As with almost every other decision, your ethics may influence which company you buy these from. If money is tight, you may be concerned only with the best price. But if you want your values to run all the way through your enterprise from the very start, you may decide to deal with an ethical supplier, such as Green Your Office which only sells products that promote ecological sustainability, social justice and fair trade principles.

6. Cut the commute

Not such an issue if you're starting out from your kitchen table, but transport to work is worth considering if you intend to rent an office or begin hiring staff. Encouraging people to use bikes or public transport can help cut pollution and congestion. If this is central to your ethical values, you could make it a defining character of your business by writing a no-car policy into your constitution (see p.124). In the last 50 years, the number of private cars in the UK has risen from approximately two million to around 25 million, so anything you can do to slim the numbers

– such as installing bicycle stands or organising a car pool scheme – can only be positive. Organisations such as Liftshare can help you put this idea into practice.

Liftshare
www.liftshare.org

Car sharing and transport information service. Match you or your employees' car journeys online with others doing the same route.

7. Use recycled stationery

The Environment Agency reports that every tonne of recycled paper saves 17 trees and 32,000 litres of water. As well as diverting paper from landfill sites and reducing the amount of chlorine used in manufacture, recycled paper is usually no more expensive to buy and of no discernibly different quality. There are many other recycled products on the market too, such as envelopes, notepads, pens, sticky notes and ink cartridges.

8. Choose ethical services

When you start up a business, you will need to choose a number of different services, such as bank accounts and insurance policies. Your ethics could influence these decisions in many ways. When you open an account for your ethical business, do you care how ethical your bank is? If not, you may only decide to look for the best interest rates and overdraft deal. But if you don't want to support a bank which may fund international arms deals, there are a number of ethical options out there.

The Co-operative Bank, for example, refuses to deal with companies that "participate in armaments, animal testing for cosmetics, nuclear power, tobacco or companies that operate in countries where human rights are disregarded". The internet-based sister to the Co-operative, Smile, the Ecology Building Society and the Dutch bank, Triodos, are other ethical banks.

Equally, if you want to source your business, property and employers liability insurance from a company that is committed to sustainable business practices, you might opt for a policy from Naturesave over less ethically conscious competitors.

Why does your choice matter? Supporting a business with similar beliefs to yourself not only adds to your own ethical credentials, it also shows your customers, and any staff, that your core values are aligned. You will also be helping another ethical business to succeed.

9. Employ clean design and technology

If you plan to launch a new product, there are many ways to incorporate your ethics from the very start. If you want to check that every stage of your design process is as environmentally friendly as possible, you could talk to DesignTrack, a free and confidential service offered by the Envirowise agency. They will send over a design advisor to look at your idea and suggest ways to reduce the environmental impact of your product over its entire lifecycle. If you have a great new "green" concept, you could even qualify for grant funding (see p.167) to get your idea off the ground.

10. Use eco-friendly packaging

If your ethical company specialises in selling fairly traded nuts and cereals, you will need to find a way to package them. As a nation, we generate some 400 million tonnes of waste annually, a figure which is growing by three per cent each year. Much of this is product packaging, frequently plastic-based and hugely polluting. It's a major environmental problem, but in recent years, there have been huge advances in biodegradable packaging. Regular plastic can be replaced by either recycled plastics or compostable plastic alternatives. Envirowise has a free downloadable guide entitled Unpack Those Hidden Savings: 120 Tips on Reducing Packaging Use and Costs.

Clean your supply chain

The supply chain is another name for the flow of materials, information and goods through a business. Selling to a customer is typically the final stage in this chain.

If you are selling sustainably produced children's toys, you may buy from a wholesaler, who in turn buys toys or materials from a manufacturer. If you provide a service (selling expertise rather than tangible products), you may have a much shorter chain.

Why does your supply chain matter? The main reason is that your business may be financially supporting other companies – with very different ethical values to your own – all the way back down the chain. It would be unfortunate for a café that proactively employs disadvantaged people and sells only Fairtrade certified drinks, to unknowingly source its tables and chairs from a furniture company that buys wood from unsustainable sources and doesn't pay its staff a living wage. But this situation could easily arise, if the café doesn't check up on its suppliers.

Besides the obvious ethical issues, there are also PR (and therefore financial) implications to guaranteeing your entire chain carries the same values as your business. If potential customers see that your suppliers have irresponsible environmental practices, it could seriously undermine your status as an ethical business.

Where to start

There are two ways of cleaning the supply chain: only choosing suppliers who already behave ethically and trying to change existing suppliers' habits.

Unless you are a very powerful customer (and even then, there's no guarantee of your influence) it can be very difficult to change the habits of a company, which in all likelihood will be bigger than you, especially if you have just started up. But it is certainly worth asking them about their credentials. Even if they aren't interested in cutting their environmental impact, you might still be able to persuade them of the cost benefits of being more sustainable.

If you are an important customer or buyer, you can think about using your clout. Supermarkets are often criticised for bullying their suppliers, but when they use their muscle to make positive changes – e.g. by reducing plastic production, as Sainsbury announced in 2006 with its "orange carrier bag" made from 33 per cent recycled plastic – they have the power to make a massive difference.

Nevertheless, even as a small company you still have the power to positively discriminate in favour of companies who have similar beliefs to your own. If a company offers great, competitively priced products and can show that workers' rights are guaranteed all the way down the supply chain, then it makes clear sense to use them over a competitor – and explain why you are using them.

There are other ways to get more involved in defining what kind of chain you want. If your products

Grimshaw: Green design

"We take our inspiration from nature," says Martin Pawlyn of architectural eco-pioneers Grimshaw. "For us, it's a fantastic storehouse of ideas."

Since designing the transparent "biome" greenhouses at the Eden Project environmental centre in Cornwall, Grimshaw has been involved in a number of equally sustainable projects. The latest is an offshore wind generator. If current tests perform as expected, a cluster of just 100 generators could outperform almost all of Britain's existing wind farms put together.

The field of architecture, Pawlyn admits, is not an obvious ethical business. Usually, new buildings are talked about as necessary evils – the focus tends to be on how to keep the negative impacts to a minimum. Grimshaw is trying to buck that trend, instead finding ways to actually *improve* the environment it aims to transform.

To make this happen, the company has developed its own environmental audit system, known as the EVA. Where many environmental systems only allow architects to check their sustainability rating after design, the new EVA tool influences the design from an early stage.

"They say most of the biggest mistakes are made on day one," says Pawlyn. "We wanted to make sure we get those fundamental decisions right from the start."

The EVA enables architects to assess a project's impact on the environment at every step of the building development. The company's emphasis on harnessing nature can yield surprising results for the client, such as huge savings in their energy bills.

Recent Grimshaw green design initiatives include installing composting tubes to turn domestic waste into heat energy to run an "eco-rainforest" visitor attraction, and using sea water to help power an innovative coastal theatre. But besides better energy efficiency and the obvious environmental benefits, Pawlyn sees another big plus in leading the field in sustainable architecture.

"Most modern architects like to be contemporary, and what could be more relevant today than having an interest in environmental issues?" he says. "I think those who ignore them will increasingly be seen as being out of date."

www.grimshaw-architects.com

are being flown in from abroad, for example, are there ways of sourcing more locally, or using more eco-friendly transport? These are core principles on which you can build your supply chain.

Put people first

Listen to the CEOs of multinational corporations talk about their success, and you are bound to hear the old chestnut: "People are our greatest asset." It's a cheesy line – not to mention empty if the workforce is actually overworked, underpaid and undervalued. But the theory is spot on.

If you're starting small, you may not have any employees for the first few months or even years. But as you expand, you will need to think about how you treat the people you recruit. Providing them with a great place to work can create a so-called "virtuous circle". As you gain recognition as an excellent employer, so the very best people, with similar ethical values, will seek you out. For companies regularly placed in "Top 50 Businesses to Work For" surveys, this circle ensures they always attract high calibre applicants.

According to the Guardian's 2006 Gradfacts survey, which analyses UK graduates' career choices, the more ethical an employer is perceived to be, the better graduates feel staff would be treated and the more attractive they are as an employer. Three out of four final year university students said they would need to feel happy with a prospective employer's ethical record to work there.

Besides simply being the right thing to do, looking after your employees will help your business in other ways too. After all, happy, motivated staff are more productive, more likely to use their own initiative and much less likely to want to leave.

Depending on your choice of legal structure (see Chapter 8: The Right Structure), many of your ethical principles may already be built into your operations. Workers' co-operatives are democratically run and entirely owned by their employees, for example. Social firms have strict guidelines about the people they employ.

But regardless of your structure, there are a host of extra initiatives you can implement to make your business a place where people simply love to work.

Transparency

If you are running an ethical business, what do you have to hide? If you are proud about the way your company operates, why not share it with the people you work with? In practice, there are many ways to incorporate this sense of openness. If you start an eco-travel business and want to make your staff really feel a part of what you're trying to do you might share with them company information that other businesses normally conceal, such as what profit you make from each eco-friendly holiday. As well as increasing their sense of "ownership" in the business, sharing information will also help them to understand the challenges and opportunities ahead for the business, and perhaps motivate them to come up with innovative suggestions. You could apply the same principle to making information open to the public. There may be some financial data you'd rather your competitors didn't see – but posting your profits (and what you intend to do with them) on your website, for example, is a great way to help your customers connect with your ethical values.

Safety

A healthy and safe workplace is fundamental to any ethical business. Giving people adequate training, the correct equipment and allowing them regular breaks – especially, for example, if they are using machinery or computer screens – is essential to creating a motivated workforce. If you run an organic apple juice company, the environmental value of your drink won't mean much if the people who run the fruit presses risk their lives in the process.

Flexibility

If you haven't taken a day off in weeks, the words "work-life balance" might sound like a mythical concept. But once you start thinking about taking on other people, you need to decide how they will work on a day-to-day basis. The regular 9-5 routine suits many companies, but perhaps you'll have other ideas. Flexible working hours or home-working options are not only better suited to certain industries or jobs, such as childcare or customer services, they can also benefit some of your staff, especially parents or people looking after elderly relatives.

You might also want to allow your staff time off to study – whether part-time or longer sabbaticals. This could be the right decision for your business too. Not only will your employees appreciate this commitment to their personal development, their new skills could also help your company in future. Smaller steps, such as allowing staff to store up holiday or carry it over to the next year, can also improve morale. Rigid, impersonal rules are a source of major discontent among employees in many larger companies. If you treat people with more respect, they will repay you with loyalty and hard work.

Diversity

If you single-handedly start and grow an eco-friendly plant nursery, who will you employ when seeding, potting, caring for and selling the plants gets too much for one person? If you feel strongly that certain people are under-represented in the workplace, this could influence your decision. A workforce from a diverse range of backgrounds can not only dismantle stereotypes, it could also create a tangible social benefit. When community bus company Hackney Community Transport recognised how few women were driving London buses, they began to actively encourage female applicants, especially from black and minority ethnic communities. More than 150 women signed up for training. Examples of staff diversity include:

▨ Age

▨ Ethnic group

▨ Sexual orientation

▨ Disability

▨ From disadvantaged areas

▨ Former offender

▨ Homeless

▨ Long-term unemployed

If you are taking on disabled staff, there may be additional access issues to consider. But these are often much simpler and less expensive than people think. The Department for Work and Pensions has written a new guide to help small employers understand the changes they can make to the workplace for disabled people.

Participation

As well as keeping staff informed about the company's performance, involving them in decision-making can also be a great way to create a genuine team spirit, increase innovation and drive your business forward. It is also an intrinsically ethical way of working. If you are involved in a managerial role, listening to the people on the ground might also throw up some new ideas and opinions you hadn't thought of. Some businesses, such as co-operatives (see p.129) have this kind of participation automatically built into their constitution, but even if you don't want to be a co-operative, you can still cherry-pick elements from this approach. If you run an ethical furniture store, for example, you could listen to everyone in your company (and even poll customers about new ideas), but still retain the autonomy to make the final decisions.

Local action

Whether sponsoring the local football team or raising money for charity fun runs, small businesses are typically much more rooted in their local communities than faceless, multinational corporations. As a local business person, you are also often in a much better position to know how best to make a valuable contribution. Employee volunteer schemes are a great way to include your staff in these ideas. From helping to build a youth club to using your professional skills to benefit community groups, staff projects can create team spirit and generate a real sense of achievement. If you want a less hands-on way to give something back, payroll giving enables you and any employees to give to any UK charity straight out of your gross salary. The Payroll Giving Centre can offer you advice.

Payroll Giving Centre
www.payrollgivingcentre.
org.uk

Reward

When it comes to rewarding your staff for a year of hard work, mince pies and cheap plonk might seem a pretty meagre pay off. But beyond the booze-fuelled mayhem that constitutes most people's Christmas office party, there are many ways to make your people feel really special. Your ethics may influence how you go about this. What might be an appropriate reward for your staff? A bonus is perhaps the least personal way of saying thank you. There are many more imaginative ways, from office camping holidays to special "personal development" funds. Here, you could ask people to explain what dream they would love to fulfil, and support the most worthy. Whether recording an album or cycling across Wales, it could also be an interesting way to discover what your employees are really passionate about.

Information centre about Payroll Giving aimed at businesses, charities and the general public, with guidance materials, resources and downloads.

Accreditation

Feeling part of an award-winning team can be a great motivator. Knowing that your business was voted best place to work in your area or won a special prize for environmental awareness means more than just a certificate. If the whole world knows your business is doing great things, your employees will be proud to come to work. There are now several annual awards which cover ethical businesses, such as the Observer Ethical Awards and Triodos Bank's Women in Ethical Business Awards. These are a great way to be recognised both for your business and your ethical credentials.

Fairness

There's not much point selling fair trade goods if you don't pay your own staff on time. Having a reliable payment structure will earn you the respect and appreciation of your employees. Regular staff reviews, clear promotion opportunities and bonus payments are additional ways to find out people's expectations, encourage commitment and reward excellence. If you set up an environmentally conscious architecture practice, ensuring that your eco-architects' wage cheques arrive promptly will assure your staff that you take *their* well-being – as well as the planet's – very seriously.

Sharing

If you have an amazing green business idea and want to grow your company as fast as possible, giving your staff shares in the business could be a big incentive for them to do a great job. But even if you're not dreaming of floating on the stock market (or if you simply want to retain full control of the business yourself), you can still give employees a sense of

Koan: Straight talking

In an industry known for corporate cover-ups and pressurised working conditions, Elaine James, MD of ethical public relations firm Koan, wanted to create a new environment, where people and principles were at the heart of the enterprise.

To start, Elaine had to define what being ethical meant to her. She decided she couldn't work with clients that she didn't believe in – even if that meant losing jobs.

"It's quite sobering when you say to the team, 'We've got over £100,000 worth of business here. Are we going to stick to our guns and not take it on?' It's very empowering."

Elaine was in just that kind of situation when a large train operating company wanted Koan to take on its PR. After initial investigation, Elaine found that the business's parent company was involved in nuclear weapons. "Even some of the people working there didn't know," she recalls. "So I had to say no. I am very open with the team. I told them it would impact on the bottom line and how much we could pay ourselves."

Nevertheless, the Manchester- and London-based company still manages to pay people well, and regularly finds itself pitching for business against the really big names of the PR world. "It's a bit like David and Goliath," Elaine smiles, "and we win because of what we do. A lot of companies have their CSR division alongside their marketing division. Being ethical is just one part of their business. With us, it's fundamental to our culture."

Besides refusing to work with unethical businesses, Koan also runs several initiatives to motivate staff, encourage teamwork and generally make its offices a fun place to work.

Elaine has also added to her legal framework. Since starting Koan from her kitchen table as a limited company, she has set up an umbrella company (Magic Bean Company Ltd), which stands above two other new strands: a charitable foundation and an enterprise initiative, which aims to encourage young social entrepreneurs in the northwest of England. Koan will give successful entrants funding and expertise to help get their business up and running.

"We are still small ourselves," says Elaine, "but we're punching above our weight. You have to start creating it, no matter how ridiculous it feels."

www.koanuk.com

ownership in the company. A "phantom" share scheme is one option. Essentially a cash bonus based on the business' performance, phantom shares don't require you to float; in fact, you can create yours from scratch – taking into account the kind of incentives you want to give your staff. If you like the sound of this, or any other kind of staff share scheme, you will need some legal advice.

Support your community

Which community do you most identify with? Depending on the nature of your business, it could be the people in your local village or an indigenous tribe in South America.

When it comes to defining your community, the area in which you trade is an obvious start. But you may have personal reasons for choosing other places: for example, where you source your supplies from, or where most of your clientele originate. Remember that you can give something back to a variety of communities and even help foster links between them all.

If you start a food distribution co-operative, you could be importing coffee from Ethiopia and working from a factory in Leeds. If you donate a percentage of your turnover to development projects in Ethiopia and to local homelessness charities in Yorkshire, you will be supporting a very diverse community.

Location, location, location

Where you set up the business can itself be an ethical choice. Many disadvantaged areas face so many difficulties because of the lack of existing business infrastructure. This creates high levels of unemployment, forces local people to travel miles looking for work and results in a variety of social problems. Simply by setting up an enterprise in these locations, you are providing work and giving something back to the local community. As an added bonus, you may also qualify for a variety of grant funding packages or be eligible to access money from an area-specific investment fund (see Chapter 9: Raising Finance).

You can take this commitment one step further by giving your community a voice in the business. Just as you might want to include employees in decision-making, can you involve local people too? Whether through shares or a seat on the board, this can reinforce your core principles. When ethical hot drinks company Cafédirect became a public company in 2004, for example, it undertook a complete overhaul of its management structure. Today, two of its 10 board members are producer partners from Tanzania and Peru. They represent the 250,000 producers from 11 different nations who supply goods to Cafédirect.

CHECKLIST ✓
People, profit and planet

- ☐ Reduce and save energy
- ☐ Buy ethically
- ☐ Use green design, packaging and technology
- ☐ Choose ethical services
- ☐ Clean your supply chain
- ☐ Create a safe, fair workplace
- ☐ Promote diversity and participation at work
- ☐ Reward employees fairly
- ☐ Define and support your community

Time and money

Another direct way to support communities is by offering them your time or facilities free of charge. As well as employee volunteer schemes, shop owners could provide shelf space to local producers or sellers, while services, such as plumbers or architects, might offer pro bono work to a local charity or faith group.

There are many other innovative gestures. Donating a set percentage of your revenue or profits to specific community regeneration projects can have a huge impact on the local area. Alternatively, you could set up your own charitable foundation and take a more hands-on role in how the money is spent. You may think this sounds like a big step for a small business, but setting up a foundation doesn't have to be complicated. You can get the basic framework in place and take it one step at a time. If this sounds appealing, the Charity Commission has a downloadable application pack.

Charity Commission

www.charity-commission.gov.uk

Regulator for charities in England and Wales, deals with registration of new charities and foundations, provides advice and support.

Making a connection

If your charitable foundation is closely aligned with the purpose of your business, an added advantage is that they could mutually support one another. If you run a fair trade fashion business, you could set up a foundation that provides grants to young designers who want to work in the developing world with fair trade producers. This could benefit the producers in your supply chain, and may also provide you with an early eye on any up-and-coming fashion talent.

If you want to use your *product* to make a difference, you could offer discounts to charitable organisations or disadvantaged communities; if you start an organic cake company, you could give away any unsold produce to local good causes.

Continuous Entertainment: On the right track

"One of the girls was 13 when she recorded her first track here," says Eve Horne, co-founder of Woolwich-based music studio and production company, Continuous Entertainment.

"Her parents didn't know she was writing songs, and when they heard she was saving her money to come to the studio, they gave her a lot of stick. But as soon as they heard the song, everything changed. It really brought the family together."

The studio that Eve and co-founder Jessica Farrar set up in 2005 is more than a music facility. Located in one of south London's most disadvantaged areas, it helps break down barriers to careers in the music industry, especially among women and minority ethnic communities.

"I grew up around here and there has never been anything for musicians," explains Eve. "We wanted to change that and help young people who don't have money to succeed."

Continuous Entertainment runs a hi-tech music workshop. Budding musicians come to record songs and learn about production. Eve and Jessica keep the fees to a minimum, and there is a 50 per cent reduction for students and people on benefits.

"It's important to make this as accessible as possible," says Eve. "We've worked with over 300 people in the 18 months we've been up and running. Lots of them have gone on to perform at local festivals."

The company was started by a £10,000 grant and £5,000 loan from the Prince's Trust. Within a year, it had won a National Business Award and come runner-up in the London Development Agency's Enterprising London awards.

Continuous Entertainment is now looking to win commercial contracts from schools, record labels and businesses. This extra capital will help the company continue to support disadvantaged groups as it moves base to Tottenham, north London.

"We want to work with even more young women," Eve says. "Many of them see music as a male-dominated world, or simply don't see past being a singer. There are so many jobs in the industry, they don't need to be scared. What we do is music, but so much of our work is about building people's confidence."

www.thelabonline.com

6 Getting Ready

IN THIS CHAPTER...

- When to ask for help
- Where to find business support
- How to access ethical specialists
- How to maximise your potential

ONCE YOU HAVE an idea of the kind of ethical business *you* want to run, it's time to turn the theory into practice. Whether you intend to start up an advertising agency or an organic bed and breakfast, many of the same practical steps will apply.

If you have any business experience, this will prove very useful. Not only might you already understand some of the fundamental issues – such as cash flow and budgeting – but any potential lenders will look on you more favourably. If you come from a voluntary sector background, you may also have many transferable skills at your disposal. Writing a complex funding application is one way of selling your organisation to a third party: a business plan is another.

But even if this is your first venture into enterprise, you have nothing to worry about. It's a myth that successful business leaders are a special breed. There is no particular kind of personality that rises to the top. Even if you have zero business background, if you get the basics right and are passionate about your beliefs, success will follow.

It can sometimes even be an advantage to know nothing about your chosen industry. Many of the world's most innovative ethical entrepreneurs have succeeded precisely because they weren't constrained by current thinking.

"If we had known about the industry before we got involved, we would have made all the wrong decisions," is a commonly heard line. Thinking in a different way to your competitors is often the very best way to develop your business.

Self-appraisal

You know what you want to achieve, but where do you start? The first step is to make an honest appraisal of your own personal strengths and weaknesses. What areas of business do you feel confident about? What skills do you think you lack? By identifying any gaps in your knowledge, you can seek out the most useful advice and save yourself time.

As an *ethical* business, you will also need to think about how your social and environmental values will impact on your everyday business decisions. If you are committed to reducing your company's carbon footprint as much as possible, for example, do you have the time and knowledge to do this all by yourself, or will you need outside expertise? If you plan to give away a percentage of your revenue to a charity in the developing world, do you understand how that may affect your profit forecast?

One of the common reasons that so many small businesses fail in their first few years is because the people running them become distracted by their "big idea". If your business is directly committed to alleviating a huge social problem, such as poverty in your local community, it can be even easier to become distracted by your goals. But if you want to realise these ambitions, you will need to be hard-nosed about the business side.

If you plan to set up an organic juice bar franchise to provide jobs for disadvantaged young people, you will inevitably spend a lot of time handling day-to-day practicalities, such as dealing with suppliers and managing your accounts. If you see yourself principally as an "ideas" person, however, and want to concentrate on going into communities, meeting young people and motivating them to get involved, you may need someone else to handle the juice bar itself from the very start.

A helping hand

Run a web search for "business support", and you'll get over a billion search results. Everyone, it seems, is trying to help you write that perfect marketing strategy, improve your business plan or boost your management skills.

Where entrepreneurs were once isolated, the problem today could be an overload of support services. From government-funded, free advice organisations to expensive business consultants, there is no shortage of well-meaning "experts" at hand. As an ethical business, you have an even greater choice. Besides the mainstream sources of support, there are several agencies who specialise in helping ethical business and "social enterprises" (see Resources).

These can be useful if you want to talk to someone who understands companies who value more than just profit. If you run a community arts enterprise, you may find that specialist social enterprise advisors will immediately "get" what you're all about. They will be used to dealing with businesses that have a strong social purpose. Unlike other advisors, they may appreciate that increasing your profit margin may not *always* be your number one priority if, for example, you would rather charge local people lower prices.

Mainstream business support can, however, help you in other ways. Sometimes you might just want a second opinion about a straightforward business decision you want to make. Other times, you may be looking for someone with expert knowledge about something you're not sure about, such as balance sheets or PR strategies.

"When we started out, we joined our nearest business centre," says Richard Reed, director of Innocent Drinks. "I would recommend that to anyone setting up their own company.

"If it's rubbish you can walk away," he adds. "If it's not, you might find something useful. Our main source of advice was speaking to existing and previous bosses and people we knew. But we definitely found useful contacts and advice at the business centre."

Different kinds of business support

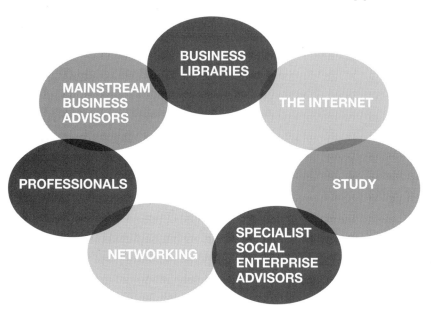

The right advice

There are many different sources of mainstream and specialist business advice throughout the UK.

Business Links are government-funded advice agencies dedicated to supporting small and medium-sized businesses. There are 42 separate Business Links spread throughout England, plus sister organisations in Wales, Northern Ireland and Scotland. Your local branch will be able to give you plenty of free general start-up business advice, but they are unlikely to have a specialist knowledge of your social and environmental impacts.

This is where specific sector advisors come to the fore. Social enterprise support organisation **SETAS** has a searchable directory of specialist business consultants, who will immediately understand your ethical values, and it has a list of training courses.

Business Link
www.businesslink.gov.uk

Government's business support network, with downloadable resources, online advice, local offices and lots of free help available.

"Mainstream business advice was a help and a hindrance to us," reflects Jonny Goldstone of Green Tomato Cars, an environmentally friendly private car hire service. "The good thing was that they challenged our ideas and made us think twice about everything. But we found they also applied traditional rules to our business without necessarily having the knowledge of how we work.

"Because they are advisors, they can also make you do unnecessary things simply in order to give you advice – like writing and re-writing business plans when you're trying to do a million other things. But overall, it was a constructive experience for us."

Local business centres often run inexpensive workshops. Once you've identified areas of weakness, this is a good place to start filling the gaps. If you start an environmentally sound plumbing business, but can't tell your profit and loss account from your balance sheet, a basic accounting course is a must. Even if you end up hiring an accountant to look after your books, a working knowledge of basic accounts is essential to stay in control of your day-to-day business. After all, if your finances spiral out of control and business plummets, your ethical principles will suffer too.

If your business has a strong technological bias, for example providing IT solutions and equipment to charities and trade unions, your local **Regional Technology Centre** (RTC) is a good source of ideas and information. RTC North, for example, focuses not only on core technology processes, but also on helping businesses find premises, access funds, expand internationally and improve manufacturing.

The **National Federation of Enterprise Agencies** (NFEA) is another UK network of support agencies, such as Local Enterprise Councils, which

SETAS
www.setas.co.uk

Social Enterprise Training And Support offers consultancy, training, advice and resources specifically about starting and growing a social enterprise.

National Federation of Enterprise Agencies

www.nfea.com

Membership body for Local Enterprise Agencies. Use the website to find your local one. Also runs a free, confidential business advice service.

Ashoka

www.ashoka.org

Global association of the world's leading social entrepreneurs, runs a venture fund for outstanding social entrepreneurs.

are aimed at all start-up and small businesses. Besides offering free professional support through its Small Business Advice website, the NFEA also runs the Business Volunteer Mentors scheme, which can put you in touch with business expert volunteers for free or heavily subsidised mentoring sessions.

Even if you have very limited funds for business support, you may not have to rely on cheap or free advice. Depending on the size of your company, you could qualify for financial help through the Learning and Skills Council's **Train to Gain** initiative. A government-funded scheme, it is designed to help small businesses access vocational education or business training. If you employ less than 50 full-time employees you may be eligible for a contribution to your wage costs. If eligible, you will receive a contribution of £5 per hour, or the actual wage for every hour, for that employee.

One resource specifically aimed at ethical business is **Ashoka**. More of an international fellowship than a regular support organisation, Ashoka aims to help the cream of socially entrepreneurial talent. The selection process is rather long and complicated, but the reward is a living stipend for an average of three years, which allows the successful candidate "to focus full-time on building their institutions and spreading their ideas". Fellows also benefit from lifelong membership of a global support network of ethical entrepreneurs and partnerships with professional consultants.

The professionals

Many of the best sources of knowledge are not business advisors, but the people who have been there and done it. Once you have identified your strengths and weaknesses, talk to as many people as possible with hands-on experience of launching a profitable business. You might be surprised at who will actually give you their time. The UK's most successful business leaders might be incredibly busy people, but chances are they will have done their fair share of begging and borrowing in their start-up years. If you are thinking about starting up a low-emission eco-chauffeur service, you might want to approach the entrepreneurs behind other ethical transport companies. Once they hear about your values, they may just be happy to share some of their wisdom.

To understand many of the specific challenges for your ethical business, you may also need to speak to people working in the same field. The aim should be to learn as much as possible about the industry, without giving too much away. After all, if another company perceives you as a direct competitor, they may not want to talk. If your aim is to launch an international volunteering agency, you might want to be careful how much you reveal if someone senior from one of the UK's larger volunteering agencies agrees to meet up.

Informal chats (and paid meetings) with accountants, lawyers and property specialists will also help you get to grips with the most complex elements of business planning. If you're leasing property, drawing up contracts, filing accounts or protecting property rights, you will almost certainly need to call in the experts.

It is a good idea to include them early on, as this may stop you making any expensive mistakes at the start. Personal recommendations are always preferable. But if you don't have any, shop around.

Ultimately it should come down to who you feel most comfortable with. There are countless stories of companies who neglected professional advice and suffered, ones who picked cheap but ineffective professionals, and others who shelled out huge amounts for very little return. Remember that if you have a strong charitable element to the business or can show that you are a social enterprise, you may be able to secure discount rates or pro bono work.

If you are a charity or trading charity (see p.135), brokering service **Pilotlight** is another great free resource. Its members, who include experienced management consultants, financial directors and senior marketing executives, volunteer their time to help charities become more sustainable and reach a wider audience.

Pilotlight
www.pilotlight.org.uk

Recruits experienced managers and experts from the private sector to work as volunteers with charities, to share their expertise.

The right site

Besides business advice, other professional services can also be vital in the early days. A website, for example, is not just a practical tool. It is how the whole world will see and judge your business.

As an ethical business, your website is especially important because you can use it to outline your social and environmental credentials. As well as explaining what your company stands for, you can also use it to show your openness and accountability by posting online information such as your accounts, any social statements and your company's environmental impact. An internet site is also a great leveller – where else can you afford similar exposure to a multinational? Hiring a professional to get your website looking perfect could be a wise investment.

Back to school?

When it comes to educational opportunities and training for ethical business, there are a growing number of options. The Skoll Centre for Social Entrepreneurship at the Oxford Said Business School, Liverpool John Moores University, the School for Social Entrepreneurs, Cambridge University's Judge Institute, Herriot-Watt University in Edinburgh, the University of East London and the Open University all offer intensive courses in social enterprise.

These are academic packages tailored specifically at the ethical business leaders of tomorrow. If you are only just starting to think about starting up and feel like you would benefit from a structured academic course, this could be the right option for you. As well as lectures and discussions on traditional business areas, such as marketing, finance and people management (all from a social enterprise perspective, of course), you will also have the opportunity to meet and listen to guest speakers from successful ethical businesses.

There are also opportunities to get involved directly in ethical enterprise. At the Oxford Said Business School, for example, four MBA students were asked to look at ways to rebuild the society of the indigenous people of Cape York, Australia, by providing support to indigenous companies. As part of their summer project, the graduates developed a strategy on how to most effectively support and grow indigenous tourism businesses.

"This has incentivised me to do things that are rewarding," says Triston Walker, one of the four students on the project. "It has provided us all with a social perspective which we will take with us in our future working careers."

As well as motivation, knowledge and confidence, these specialist courses can also help you to meet many other like-minded people and share ideas. Who knows, you may one day end up doing business with each other.

Maximising your potential

Making contacts is an invaluable exercise for new entrepreneurs. Here, Heather Wilkinson, director of Striding Out, a support network for young ethical entrepreneurs, reveals the value of networking, coaching and mentoring:

Striding Out
www.stridingout.co.uk

Business support network for young people, aged 18-30, with enterprising ambitions, offering training, networking, coaching and events.

British Chamber of Commerce
www.chamberonline.co.uk

Claims to be the voice of British business, and hosts lots of useful resources and directories for business start-ups.

Networking

"Having a robust and dynamic network of support and experts around you is the basis of any successful business. In a recent survey of 200 entrepreneurs, networking was rated as the most valuable factor for learning. That's because it enables you to:

1. Tap into additional experience and skills across industry sectors.

2. Connect with other entrepreneurs to share knowledge and contacts.

3. Learn from more established entrepreneurs to gain inspiration, knowledge and mentoring.

4. Connect with like-minded people to discuss experiences and combat isolation.

5. Meet future clients, suppliers or business partners.

But remember, it's the quality, not quantity, of your connections that counts.

Coaching

Business coaches focus on your personal and professional development. They can help solve problems and identify opportunities.

Running a business, especially on your own, can be like running on a treadmill. You're not sure when to get off as there is always more to do. Coaching sessions can provide a space for you to step out of life for a moment and reflect on the bigger picture.

It is important to find a coach who is in tune with your business and social values. It should be someone you have a good rapport with and confidence to share concerns, and who has suitable business acumen and understanding.

To maximize the value of the relationship, identify three specific goals or tasks that you want to achieve in advance. During the introductory session, explain your circumstances and what you need from them. Then set a realistic time frame to achieve these goals. Finally, agree dates for future sessions and set aside a time to review your relationship and progress.

Mentoring

Mentors are individuals with established business and/or industry experience. Their role is to give advice, challenge concepts and provide you with contacts. They are more business-task orientated than coaches.

CHECKLIST ✓
Getting ready

- [ ] Evaluate your personal strengths and weaknesses
- [ ] Exploit mainstream business support
- [ ] Tap into specialist social enterprise advice
- [ ] Take useful business courses
- [ ] Seek relevant professional advice
- [ ] Start to build up a business network
- [ ] Consider coaching and mentoring

When choosing a mentor, identify someone who will complement your weaknesses. It is important to identify the business strengths/expertise that you want them to provide – whether industry (e.g. fashion) or skill-specific (e.g finance).

It is important to anticipate the number of hours of expertise you require and what they can offer. Equally important is to consider whether it is free or paid mentoring. You should also agree in advance on your expectations of what they can offer."

StreetShine: Skilling up

StreetShine is a young company dedicated to helping homeless people find mainstream employment. All of its employees – or "shiners" – receive training in shoe shining, and work daily shifts at blue-chip companies in London. They earn a regular income, have a bank account and ultimately the chance to start up their own franchise.

Although it reinvests 100 per cent of profits back into the business, StreetShine is structured as a regular limited company. Nevertheless, when Simon Fenton-Jones became chief executive in 2004, he found that the business's strong ethical credentials and close links to homelessness charities meant he was able to call in an impressive number of favours. As a result, he has brought a wealth of expert knowledge into the business.

"A blue-chip company's corporate social responsibility policy works two ways for us," he explains. "It's one way for us to approach them for business, but it can also give us access to their expertise. We've had situations where a company hasn't wanted our shiners, but said they could support us in other ways."

To date, StreetShine has received pro bono help from several major corporations. Global information company Reuters has delivered a customer-care training programme. Accountancy firm KPMG handles the company's payroll, while law firm Lovells has provided legal advice.

In the beginning, Simon paid for a professional shoe shiner to teach him how to treat and look after shoe leather. He and his team now pass that knowledge on to new recruits. This, and the free customer-care manual from Reuters, means that StreetShine has slashed its training costs.

Simon has also received free advice through charity support organisation Pilotlight. Expert mentors have helped him with financial management, as well as marketing and communications strategies. He also enrolled on the School for Social Entrepreneurs course to learn more about running a business focused both on profit and principles.

Another major source of assistance has been StreetShine's board, which includes experienced heads both in big business and the homelessness sector. "It's great to have so many contacts at the end of the phone," says Simon. "Setting up a business can be a lonely experience, but I know I've got fantastic support."

StreetShine began with start-up funding of £50,000, and the same figure in loan funding, from the Glimmer of Hope UK trust. It has since won an £80,000 business development grant from the Esmée Fairbairn Foundation, but after two years of trading, the company has cut its grant dependency in half.

"In two years, we're aiming to be financially self-sufficient," says Simon, "I'm confident the business will grow exponentially. We've just started offering our services to smaller companies, and are also trialling a car wash business. This is just the tip of the iceberg."

www.streetshine.com

7 Business Basics

IN THIS CHAPTER...

- How to turn a clean profit
- How to define your ethical identity
- What your market wants
- How to build your business case

THERE IS NO one right way to set up a business. For some people, it starts as a hobby. One day, they wake up and that personal passion has somehow taken over and translated into the blueprint for an ethical enterprise.

Whatever your ethical business, there is a certain amount of basic business skills you will need to get to grips with to make your idea work long-term. The good news is that – untangled from unnecessary jargon – those skills are easy to understand and implement.

For many first-time entrepreneurs, the term "business plan" is a source of much unnecessary worry. Admittedly, the prospect of hours spent drafting and refining a long, technical document is far from appealing. But the truth is that much of the ordinary thinking you need to do to prepare your business will slot right into the plan. Simply by doing your basic research and getting a clear idea of how your ethical enterprise will work, you will have much of it already written.

The right track

It doesn't matter how well intentioned your beliefs, the normal rules of business will still apply to your company. After all, your business will only be able to make a social difference if it succeeds financially and that means meeting market demands just like any regular business.

If you value your social and environmental goals above all else, you may not like the sound of traditionally materialistic concepts, such as marketing or promotion. But these are essential components of any successful enterprise, and you will need to embrace them. It is unrealistic to think that people will buy your product or service simply because it's good for the planet. You will have to get every part of the business right if you want to stand head and shoulders above the competition.

Often you will even need to run a better business than your rivals. Depending on your ethical policies, you may be making decisions that will negatively affect your cash flow or balance sheet. To compete on quality and price, you will therefore have to think of innovative ways to get the very best out of your business.

Turning a clean profit

"I am in business to make friends and serve the community. Profit for me is by the way. One has to make profit and balance the books, otherwise the business will go bust, but profit is not the main motivation. Profit oils the wheels, but the purpose of operating the wheels is not to consume oil but to produce something for people."
Eco-pioneer and author, Dr Satish Kumar

Profit has a bad reputation. It's not hard to see why. While British supermarkets post multi billion-pound profits every year, small farmers continue to go out of business in record numbers. It is hardly fair that directors of mega corporations are awarding themselves mammoth rises, while minnows in the supply chain are squeezed into bankruptcy.

But while profit often hits the headlines for all the wrong reasons, it *is* a fundamental driver for all entrepreneurial businesses. Valuing social and environmental returns is what sets ethical businesses apart from the rest, but no enterprise can afford to neglect profit.

If you sell local, organically produced chutneys, the farming communities you support won't thank you if you don't create enough business to keep your company afloat for the long-term.

Not for profit?

Many businesses and charities make a lot of fuss about being "not for profit". But what they usually mean is that they don't pay out profits to owners or shareholders. After subtracting their costs, they will still hope to have a positive figure in the net income column. In other words, they make profit. Crucially, this money is either fed back into the organisation, or given to a charitable foundation.

How much can you earn as the owner of an ethical business? In the first few years, theoretical questions like this are unlikely to trouble you; most start-up entrepreneurs would be happy to cover their costs. But looking to the medium- and long-term, there is no single answer. Bosses of huge multinationals will often point to their multi billion-dollar turnovers, thousands of employees and contributions to a nation's economic wealth to justify fat cat salaries. If your choice of legal structure doesn't put any controls over your earnings, you too will be able to decide how much to take out, and how much to share.

Doing the right thing

To begin with, take as little as you can. Young businesses are notoriously cash-hungry; without the economies of scale that big companies can rely on, you may have to pay high prices for goods and services, and may struggle to find anyone willing to give you credit. It is therefore sensible to survive on the minimum and plough as much revenue-generated money as possible back into your business. Taking the cash out straightaway could seriously hamper potential for growth.

But once you are established, healthy annual profits are something to celebrate, not be ashamed of. This sentiment was echoed by Steve Case, co-founder of AOL, founder of enterprise fund Revolution, and chairman of The Case Foundation, in an interview with the Wall Street Journal in 2005.

"Whether you're running a business that also

serves a valuable social objective, or running a non-profit that earns part of its income through viable commercial activity, purpose and profit aren't zero-sum, they're mutually reinforcing."

Innocent Drinks is cagey about its precise profit figures, but its three founder directors each reportedly earn £120,000 a year. It may sound like a lot, but many comparable market leaders in other industries will take home far bigger salaries. Besides, Innocent has implemented strong social and environmental policies throughout the business, and contributes 10 per cent of all its profits to charity. If it didn't do this, the directors could certainly be earning much more. Should you be fortunate enough to arrive at a similar position, deciding what is a reasonable amount will always be a personal choice. Running an ethical business, however, is not about wearing sackcloth and eating bread and water. Above all, it is about fairness.

Choosing a name

What are you going to call your business? Choosing a name is a personal decision, but remember that your name will also be the very first thing that people judge you on. As an ethical business, you might therefore want your name to convey some of your social and environmental values.

Private hire car companies, for example, typically focus either on their family origins (e.g. Addison Lee) or their efficient service (e.g. Express Cabs). But when Tom Pakenham and Jonny Goldstone were wondering what to call their electric hybrid, low-emission cab firm, they decided to incorporate their strong environmental beliefs into the name, and came up with Green Tomato Cars. As well as

Blue Ventures: Success on a shoestring

★ *Blue Ventures is an award-winning, non-profit distributing company dedicated to marine research and conservation in Madagascar. Its expeditions are run in close collaboration with local communities and aim to leave a lasting legacy. In 2003, Alasdair Harris set up Blue Ventures as a company limited by shares. Its constitution guarantees profits are fed back into a registered charity arm of the enterprise. The company earns money by charging members of the public to join its dive trips.*

On setting up

"We were stepping out into the unknown. We initially launched the business website when we were at university. Later that year we had our first paying customers, and within two years, we'd gone from an idea to a viable business. We have been playing catch up, but we're now in our first year of profit."

On life as an ethical entrepreneur

"Turning down other opportunities was a challenge. Deciding not to become a management consultant like all my mates, and having to live on nothing for a year was a major stress. It takes its toll on your finances and your relationships. In the beginning, we couldn't afford to pay ourselves and shared a room together for six months."

On finances

"We have never taken a loan or overdraft. We had nothing to guarantee against, and it never interested us anyway. We put in the remainders of our student overdraft: £500. If there's a story to tell about Blue Ventures, it's about sheer determination. We've not had anyone bank-rolling us. We've run marathons, done fundraisers to get the money in. And we wasted a lot. In the early days, we were really fleeced by professional services; lawyers and accountants who took advantage of our naivety and overcharged us."

On marketing

"Blue Ventures doesn't have a marketing budget. We rely on begging newspapers to give us free coverage, and we pay commission to some websites and do cross-advertising on [sister organisation] Travel Roots, an eco-tourism company. The web is our biggest marketing tool. If you see an ad in the paper, we haven't paid for it."

www.blueventures.org

being quirky and memorable, it also clearly aligns their business with nature.

Whatever name you choose, try to keep it short and inclusive. In other words, don't let your name limit what you can do – after all, you never know how the business might evolve. If you want to start an online ethical gift shop for girls, calling yourself "Planet Princess" could cause you problems if you decide later on to create a boy's line. A more generic name could be the answer.

Test out your ideas among friends; especially ones you know will give you an honest opinion. Once you're happy, check the website domain name is available, and then visit Companies House's homepage. There's a search engine, so you can see if anyone has beaten you to it.

Companies House
www.companieshouse.
gov.uk

Government's register of companies, with downloadable information and searchable database. You'll get to know them very well soon enough.

Mission statement

"I was always told if you can't explain your business idea in one sentence to your granny then you don't have a good business idea."
Richard Reed, Innocent Drinks

When you communicate with customers or suppliers, it is important for them to know exactly who you are. Your mission statement – a snappy, upbeat summary of the business – can help you achieve just that. It can be more than one sentence, but should be concise and easily understood.

As an ethical business, it's also a great opportunity for you to highlight your ethical aims and values. For anyone who visits your website, for example, a well-written mission statement can quickly and firmly establish your credentials as an ethical business.

What to include

When thinking about your statement, try to include the answers to the following questions:

1. Who are you?

2. What do you do?

3. What do you stand for?

4. Why are you doing it?

solarcentury: mission statement

"Solarcentury is in business for a purpose: to help create a cleaner world and a sustainable future. Our aim is to revolutionise the global energy market.

"The sun bathes the earth in an incredible amount of energy – in a day, enough arrives to power the whole world for several years.

Humanity can now effectively harness the power of the sun. The 21st century must be the solar century.

"We envisage solar systems on the roof of every building, backed up by a family of other micro renewables, supplying clean power and achieving deep cuts in emissions.

"As the global market for renewable energy grows, thousands of jobs will be created in research, installation and manufacturing. A sustainable future is within our reach, in this generation."

www.solarcentury.com

Red Ochre: Getting it right

★ *Uday Thakkar, director of London-based business consultancy Red Ochre, specialises in advising ethical businesses. Here are his top 10 tips for entrepreneurial success:*

Vision

Create and hold on to your vision. You may have to change how you get there but don't become distracted from your ultimate goal. Make sure you can communicate your vision simply and effectively.

Value

Rigidly stick to the values that you create. Make sure everyone in your organisation knows the values and lives by them. Communicate your values to everyone you engage with. Never make promises you can't keep.

Attitude

Success requires hard work. Believe in yourself and your project, don't give up. Always remain positive and retain a sense of humour. Make each day exciting and fun – enjoy yourself! A great attitude is mirrored throughout an organisation and attracts customers. Do to others as you would have them do to you.

Team

Build a good supportive team around you; make sure they compensate your weaknesses. Employ people more talented than you. Build the team patiently to be sure you have the right people. Keep the team as small as possible; subcontract where you can. Always make sure that the team is paid, because unpaid talent exits rapidly. Be open and honest with your team.

Focus

Listen to your customers. Don't be arrogant or make assumptions. Make sure that everyone in the organisation is welcoming and polite. Assist the customer to the correct solution. Follow up and respond to customer comments. Become a customer champion.

Delivery

Practise what you preach. Deliver what you say you will, or better still, go the extra mile and give more than is expected. Remember, little extras can make all the difference, and are what you will be remembered by.

Identity

Create a bright and bubbly identity. Be quirky. Come across as being bigger than you are. Choose easy to remember names, logos and designs. Rigidly use the identity on everything you generate. Ensure that your public interface (reception/office/showroom/website) look great. Constantly promote yourself, internally as well as externally.

Cash

Knowing your cash position intimately will allow you to anticipate problems or seize opportunities. Make sure you understand the difference between profit and cash flow. Know, measure and control your costs. Create a pricing policy that generates profits. Don't be embarrassed to chase those who owe you money. If paying suppliers is proving a problem, keep talking to them. Absence of communication causes panic. Agree an honest repayment schedule and keep to it.

Network

Network like mad. Seize every opportunity to meet new people. Networks generate new ideas, new customers, new opportunities, new staff and act as an early warning system. Carry business cards with you at all times. Don't be shy.

Innovate

Don't rest on your laurels. Keep an eye on your competitors and keep ahead of them. Constantly seek to improve what you have: often the small changes are the winning strategies.

www.redochre.org.uk

Ethical profile

Is there an existing market for your business? What kind of people are most likely to buy your product or service? How can you find the most ethical suppliers? To find out the answers to these and other questions, you will need to conduct some market research.

If you want to set up an ethical business in an otherwise predominantly purely profit-driven industry, such as a socially responsible IT firm, you may also want to focus your research on *ethical enterprise*. How else can you know if your core values will appeal to customers?

To find out about national ethical consumer spending, take a look at the Co-operative Bank's annual Ethical Consumerism Report. It can be downloaded

Co-operative Bank
www.co-operativebank.co.uk

The biggest high-street ethical bank, with downloads online of its annual Ethical Consumerism Report. This is a useful resource for your research and business plan.

▸

Ethical Junction

www.ethical-junction.org

Very thorough online database of ethically motivated companies, in all sorts of fields and industries.

▸

Ethical Consumer Research Association

www.ethicalconsumer.org

Online information and commercial research service on companies, their ethical practices and standards, as well as a consumer magazine.

free from the bank's website. Daily newspapers and specialist publications, such as Ethical Consumer magazine, also frequently run features identifying the most ethical operators in a particular sector, and the successes they have enjoyed.

As well as helping you to understand spending habits, this research may also enable you to measure any existing competition. If you're looking to compile a list of companies which share similar social and environmental values to your own business, for example, websites such as Ethical Junction publish updated lists broken down into industry and geographical region too. If you want even more detail, the Ethical Consumer Research Association can provide you with in-depth ethical analyses of a particular business sector. Evaluating the success (or failure) of these ethical operators may help you to understand if there is room in the market for your business idea.

This information can also be useful if you are looking to source suppliers. If you plan on starting an ethical garden design business, you may want to find a list of companies who sell fair trade flowers and wood from sustainably managed forests.

DIY research

You don't have to rely on existing information, however. If you want to find out first hand how an industry ticks, you could always ask the experts. If they like your approach, existing bosses may not only share top tips on how to plan and run your business, they may also let you in on their favourite suppliers and the latest industry trends.

Another way to discover this kind of information is to get stuck in. If you are thinking about giving an

Tip... Add to your ethical portfolio

★ Cornwall-based company Wildlife didn't set out to be an ethical business. Two years ago, in the face of growing competition, the outdoor clothes retailer decided to launch its own brand, Seasalt, to try and increase profitability.

But when it came to planning the new label, directors Neil, Leigh and David Chadwick also began to think about the environmental impact of their new brand. According to the World Health Organisation, the use of pesticides kills 20,000 agricultural workers every year. In 2005, the brothers decided to use only organic cotton in their new brand.

"It was a high-risk strategy," explains Neil, "but I personally felt it was the right thing to do."

And the family business didn't want to stop there. Later that year, Seasalt became the first fashion brand in the UK to be Soil Association certified. "That really raised the profile of the business," says Neil. "It gave us some great PR."

As the demand for Seasalt has grown, so the business faces interesting dilemmas about the other clothes brands it currently stocks. "I'm very aware of the situation," says Neil. "When it comes to our ethics, we want a coherent message, but obviously we're not big

enough to walk in and tell them how to do their business. But hopefully as our own brand grows, our dependency on others will reduce. That will give us more control."

Wildlife is certainly moving in the right direction. It currently sells 90,000 units of Seasalt clothing per year, and continues to expand its ethical portfolio.

In 2006, the award-winning company took yet another step forward by using Fairtrade certified organic cotton, guaranteeing both environmental benefits and better wages for the farmers who supply the fabric.

www.wildlifeonline.com

existing service an innovative environmental twist, you could take your market research one step further by actually working at a non-green competitor and learning how the industry ticks (see Going undercover, p.103).

When it comes to finding out what *consumers* want, a less strenuous method is to source your own market research. If you want to start up a socially responsible wedding shop, you could go out and ask potential customers for their opinions on your idea. The Start Ups website has some good free advice on how to write a questionnaire. When you approach people, you will need to explain just what makes your business different to competitors in the marketplace, such as your commitment to fair trade principles, and ask them whether that would affect their shopping habits. Would customers in your area be prepared to pay more for a wedding dress, for instance, if they knew it was produced fairly, and the fabric hadn't been treated with pesticides or bleach?

Start Ups
www.startups.co.uk

Comprehensive and free information for starting your own business. Little on ethical enterprise, but the resources here are invaluable for all small businesses.

Business plans

A mission statement helps you to explain your business idea in just a few seconds. But if you want to show someone in detail just what makes your company tick, you need something much more substantial. Writing a business plan can also be an incredibly useful experience for you. With regular updating, it will accurately chart your business journey – and be an invaluable resource for spotting strengths and weaknesses.

As an ethical business, it is also a great opportunity to set down your values and beliefs in detail. Explaining your core purpose is not only relevant for anyone who may have invested in your business, it will also be of interest to any potential future lenders. If you want to take out a loan, for example, this is your chance to show how your principles and profits are mutually reinforcing – convincing the bank that your business is a safe bet.

Green Tomato Cars: Going undercover

The brainchild of two former city lawyers, pioneering minicab business Green Tomato Cars is turning a traditionally eco-unfriendly industry on its head. But the university friends' dream of starting up an ethical company might have floundered were it not for some innovative research.

When Tom Pakenham and Jonny Goldstone launched their business in spring 2006, they knew they had a great idea. With a fleet comprised entirely of electric hybrid Toyota Prius cars – reportedly one of the world's most environmentally friendly cars – Green Tomato Cars aimed to be the greenest cab company in the market. All drivers are trained in customer service, and they are no more expensive to hire than a normal cab.

Theirs might seem a simple idea, but Tom began the groundwork on the business nearly two years before the company launch. "In October 2004, I quit my job and began researching the whole private hire business," he says. "I did a variety of things, but I knew I really needed to understand the industry. So I took a job driving a minicab for two different companies. That was a key piece of research."

As well as learning the practicalities of cab driving, Tom also wanted to get an insight into the day-to-day company management. "I spoke to as many of the right people as I could, but it was quite a closed business," he admits. "There's only so much you can learn from the cab. I wanted to work in the control room to see how that all worked, but [with no relevant experience], no one would give me the job."

Nevertheless, Tom's undercover work paid off. "There are some industries that have quite a simple business model, like a shop: buy for one, sell for two," he explains. "Others are more complex – and the car business is that. There is so much to consider: the basic call centre, the drivers, the cars, both people and vehicle management, and all the admin. There are quite a few layers involved and working in the business definitely helped me to understand that."

After a year of research, Tom decided that Green Tomato Cars was a viable business. Jonny quit his job and joined in. Since launching on 1 March 2006, they have expanded their initial fleet to 35 cars and now operate across the whole of central and west London.

www.greentomatocars.com

If you are trying to run an environmentally low-impact marketing company, you can show what you have achieved both in terms of reduced carbon dioxide and waste emissions *as well as* costs saved from heating bills and refuse.

Your ethical policies will also help to explain certain business decisions, which might otherwise be misinterpreted. If you buy fair trade goods or have set up your own fair trade arrangements with producers, you may be charging more for your products than many of your competitors. If your research shows that this is what consumers want – and your sales figures back this up – you can prove that your ethical values are justified from both a social *and* a financial perspective. Your business plan is where to set this out.

A typical business plan might include the following information:

■ **Executive summary**

■ **Business overview:** What is your core business idea; how is your company structured; what makes it special?

■ **Market and competition:** What is the need for your business? Evaluation of your market, the competition, and the ethical marketplace.

■ **Ethical statement:** What are your core social and environmental values; why are they important to your business; how do they affect your business decisions; what impact will they have on your income and profits?

■ **Sales and marketing strategy:** How does your business intend to generate income?

■ **Operations:** How will you set up the business; what do you need, e.g. office space, equipment?

■ **Management:** Who runs the business? About you: what skills do you have; what is your background?

■ **Financials:** Your financial targets (including cash-flow forecasts) and your assumptions, e.g. what would happen if your sales were 10 per cent, 20 per cent, 50 per cent below target and your costs were 10 per cent, 20 per cent above target?

■ **Investment proposition/opportunity:** Who owns the business; how much money are you asking for; how will it be used; how will it be paid back?

Tip... Defy conventional business wisdom

 Ethical fashion company People Tree works with 70 fair trade groups in 20 developing countries. This is not the most cost-effective way to run its operations. Three weavers in Bangladesh, for example, can hand-weave up to 30 metres of cotton a day. Three power looms are much more pollutant, but they can weave nearly 100 metres of cotton and require just one supervisor to run. On cost alone, the machines are the best choice, but People Tree's commitment to helping marginalised people work their way out of poverty and minimising carbon emissions means that they choose to use hand weavers. It is inaccurate, however, to write this off as a total loss of income. Fair trade principles are an integral part of People Tree's ethical mix and add real value to the brand's appeal.

www.peopletree.com

You can find dozens of books about how to write a business plan, and hundreds more websites offering business plan templates. None will fit your company perfectly, but it can be helpful to compare the different approaches. Figuring out what isn't relevant to your business will help you avoid doing unnecessary work.

As a rule of thumb, your business plan should be between 15 and 30 pages long. Bank managers and investors see a lot of business plans. The trick is to keep them concise without skimping on the key details. Go too short and you're not giving them enough evidence of your trustworthiness, especially if you're looking for a serious amount of money. Write an epic and they will lose interest.

Stocking up

To get your business off the ground, you may need to find a new office, source stock or buy new equipment. The Business Link website has practical sections on sourcing premises, organising contracts with suppliers, and planning inventory controls, which will help you with many of the big issues.

When it comes to finding office space, ethical enterprises have more options than solely profit-oriented companies. If you start a business which creates jobs for a disadvantaged community, for example, you could qualify for assistance from the Ethical Property Company, an investment group which buys and develops buildings for ethical businesses.

According to its criteria, if you make

Ethical Property Company
www.ethicalproperty.co.uk

National property developer offering office space at reasonable rates and on flexible tenancy terms to ethical businesses.

a positive difference to either "the environment, overseas and community development, human, civil and women's rights, peace, homelessness and refugee (or) minority issues", you could qualify for reasonably priced, flexible tenancy office space. If you only need a single desk, its Spaces for Change programme could even give you workspace rent-free for a few months while you concentrate on getting your business up and running.

Ethical suppliers

Once you have established a base, you may then want to make your company's supply chain as ethical as possible. If you don't just want to be an ethical cog in an otherwise amoral machine, you can actively favour business partners who share similar social and environmental principles to you (see p.61). When it comes to negotiations, however, don't assume that your ethical principles will bring you any favours. Indeed, you will need to be just as vigilant for con merchants, as fair trade shop Mondomundi discovered when it opened in 2006. "We ended up firing the shop-fitters," says director Phil Soulsby. "I had found the perfect shop for our business, but when I wanted to get it fitted out, I was quoted £40,000. In the end, we did it ourselves for £5,000. Having an extra £35,000 is always handy."

A fair price

Prices are usually controlled by the market. When you need to set yours, a simple method is to consider what you could reasonably charge, and then work out your costs. By comparing the two, you can calculate if this would give you a sufficient profit; and if not, what

Price to pay?

 There are plenty of reasons why running an ethically minded company can make good business sense, but be prepared for some additional costs too.

Many products are cheap precisely because the companies that produce them behave unethically, denying their employees decent working conditions, or forcing their suppliers to accept unreasonably low wages. If your business is based on sounder principles, you may have to take the corresponding financial hit. Having to pay more will make it that much harder for you to compete on price. But asking customers to pay more – especially if you have zero marketing budget and your competitors have an entire CSR department devoted to spinning an "ethical" image to the public – is a risky strategy.

"Being ethical *will* cost you more," says Glenn Slade, MD of Green Glass, an award-winning eco-company, which turns used bottles into colourful jewellery and glassware. "So if you want to succeed, you've got to be better than an ordinary business. A lot of social enterprises behave as if they don't belong to the real world. They think that as long as they are doing something good, they'll be all right. But it just doesn't work like that."

Ethical companies such as People Tree, which creates and sells fairly traded fashion, have to work extra hard to succeed. Unlike most of its competitors, People Tree pays the people who make its clothes long before the company receives the product. This has a major impact on cash flow. In addition, there is a high risk – and cost – involved in its policy of working with isolated communities in poor countries, who have only a limited infrastructure. If something goes wrong, it's People Tree that takes the punches, and risks losing customer loyalty.

"Fair trade is very unpredictable," says company founder Safia Minney. "When some of our suppliers in Bangladesh lost their homes in flooding, we weren't just working to provide them with relief supplies. We also had to account for the disruption and effects of late delivery on the business as well."

you might need to do to achieve it.

A common mistake among young businesses is to overlook or underestimate some of the less obvious outgoings, such as interest on bank loans or insurance. Remember, your final price has to reflect all of your costs.

As an ethical business, the nature of your product may already have a strong influence on your prices. Alternatively, you may run a service, such as an ethical media consultancy, and set different prices for different customers, offering discounts to charities or specific members of the community.

However you work with price, it is important to be realistic. The first few years are traditionally the toughest for any small business, and achieving a decent margin early on could be critical for your long-term business survival.

It is easy to assume that customers will be prepared to pay more for your product or service simply because of your social or environmental principles. While this may be the case, most successful ethical entrepreneurs warn against that kind of thinking.

You may sometimes find it simply impossible to price-match the competition, especially if they enjoy better economies of scale or are less concerned about their environmental impact. But the best-case scenario is always to equal or beat the competition on price and quality.

CHECKLIST ✓
Business basics

- ☐ Understand your goals
- ☐ Create a winning name and mission statement
- ☐ Start researching your market
- ☐ Understand your ethical profile
- ☐ Write your business plan
- ☐ Organise your stocks and supplies
- ☐ Set the right price

8 The Right Structure

IN THIS CHAPTER...

- When to stay unincorporated
- How to create a company
- When to choose a different form
- How to make your structure more ethical
- When to register as a charity

WHEN IT COMES to deciding what legal form your business should take, there is no shortage of choice. Indeed, the number and variety of different legal structures available can be overwhelming. Remember, however, that this diversity only reflects the many innovative ways in which people have approached the idea of ethical business. It's certainly not a new concept – entrepreneurs have been meeting social, ethical and environmental goals for centuries. The result is a rich mix of forms, each with its own advantages and disadvantages.

So what exactly is a structure? Put simply, it's the legal framework for your entire business. Your choice will determine whether your enterprise is a company, a charity or a not-for-profit. It will also determine who is the boss, whether you have board members, trustees, and a lot more besides.

Perhaps you have not given much thought to legal structures. Most businesses in the UK are registered as limited companies, and there's nothing to stop you doing the same. It is fast, easy and cheap. But before applying to Companies House, the official register of UK companies, it's worth at least considering the different options. Many limited companies are designed to meet the needs of enterprises solely concerned with maximising profit. If this is only one of your goals, a different structure may be better for what you are planning. Indeed, some legal forms have been specifically designed for ethically minded enterprises.

The big issues

 There are three fundamental questions at the heart of all ethical businesses. Answering these will help you find the best legal structure for your enterprise:

Who will be responsible for running the company?

The jargon "governance" simply refers to who has control of the business. When you're setting up a small business, you might want 100 per cent freedom. If you're committed to co-operative principles, you will be more disposed to sharing the decision-making process. Each legal form has different implications for governance. Much will depend on your personal feeling. A non-executive board, for example, could either be seen as a help (ensuring you meet your ethical goals) or a hindrance (interfering in your decisions).

How do you intend to generate income?

There are many ways to source the money you will need to run the business. Personal savings, generating revenue from sales, bank loans, grants and shares are the most common methods, but there are other options too. Your choice of legal structure may restrict your options, so think carefully which sources of finance will be most relevant.

What do you want to do with your profits?

Every business should aim to make a profit. The big question is what you do with yours. For some ethical enterprises, giving away all or some of their profits is an integral part of how they operate. Others will split the money between bosses and/or employees and shareholders. If this includes you, remember that some legal forms prevent any profit from being taken out of the business.

Social enterprise

As you plan, research and set up your business, you may come across the term "social enterprise". But what is it? Are you one? If a grant award or specialist support service is open to social enterprises, you will want to know.

Social enterprise is not a legal term, but it is often used to describe ethical businesses. One common definition is "a business with primarily social objectives whose surpluses are principally reinvested for that purpose in the business or community".

If that sounds like you, then congratulations: you are a social enterprise. But it is worth knowing there is some disagreement about the amount of profits that are reinvested to qualify as a social enterprise (i.e. what does "principally reinvested" really mean?). Some people insist on 100 per cent, others say 50 per cent or more. Others believe that all ethically minded businesses are worthy of the term, regardless of the percentage.

The most dynamic social enterprises in the UK don't lose any sleep about it. People like Stephen Sears, chief executive of the ECT Group, are far too busy running successful, multi million-pound turnover businesses. His social enterprise started out as a small community transport organisation, providing local bus travel for charities and funded predominantly by short-term grants. He and his team have since transformed ECT into a highly successful entrepreneurial business that, today, is not just one of London's leading community transport organisations; it is also the largest community recycling organisation in the country and has recently added a railway line and railway engineering business to its operations. At the start of 2006, it had a turnover of £40 million and was employing 900 staff.

"Social enterprises apply remarkable levels of energy, business skills, passion and innovation to change people's lives in hugely diverse ways – from recycling to restaurants, health services to third-world poverty," explains Tim West, editor of Social Enterprise magazine. "They combine real entrepreneurship and social justice to create the kind of business that makes a real difference."

Like all ethical businesses, social enterprises come in different shapes and sizes. Whether you want to start a local arts organisation that helps people with mental health problems, or an ethical micro-loan scheme for victims of loan sharks, if your business is set up to deliver a social purpose, then you're a social enterprise.

There are several advantages to the name tag. Some organisations open their grant awards to charities and social enterprises, so you might be eligible. You could also take advantage of specialist support resources. Social Enterprise Coalition's website and Social Enterprise magazine both publish practical advice and inspiring stories of other businesses, who also value principles and profit. Many of the people behind these organisations have seen hundreds of businesses successfully blend entrepreneurship with social values. They will have invaluable advice to share.

Getting it right

What is the right legal structure for your business? Making the right choice will help you in many ways. It can affect how you make decisions, raise finance and share profits.

On the surface, how you behave as a business might appear much more important than your structure. But

Social Enterprise Coalition
www.socialenterprise.org.uk

Umbrella body for member organisations in the social enterprise sector, which supports and represents their work, influences national policy and promotes best practice.

your legal form will create the framework for *how* you can behave. Not only could it help you to access certain kinds of funding, or prove to others that you have a clear social purpose, it can also enshrine your ethical beliefs into a constitution. Once you've done this, you can then concentrate on putting the theory into practice. We will be looking at the legal forms below in this chapter:

Choosing a legal structure

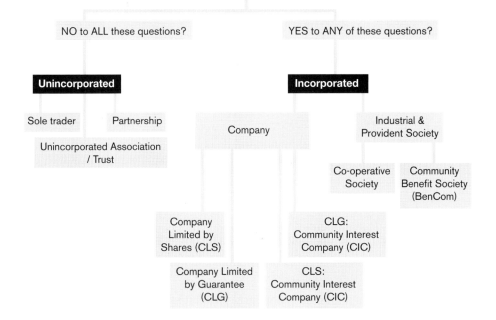

From Keeping it Legal, © *Bates, Wells & Braithwaite, reproduced with kind permission.*

Staying unincorporated

If you're starting small, the first decision is whether you need to create a company at all. Being unincorporated effectively means you (and any partners) are the business. You don't create a separate legal entity. One benefit of doing this is that you won't need much finance to begin trading, and being unincorporated also allows you to test different ways of developing the business before deciding on a final structure. If you don't need to find extra capital, take on staff or move into property in the short term, staying unincorporated offers a hassle-free starting point. Your business will be less heavily regulated than a limited company, and you won't need to register or file annual accounts with Companies House. You will also be taxed individually (not as a company), and pay any tax in arrears rather than upfront.

How many people will be involved in the earliest stages of your business? If it's just you, staying unincorporated means being a sole trader. If there is more than one of you, you could form a partnership – another unincorporated form. Partnerships are traditionally how many solicitors' practices have operated – although several have now become Limited Liability Partnerships (see p.117). If you are sharing the enterprise with someone else, it is a good idea to ask a lawyer to draw up a partnership agreement, setting out who is responsible for what and how profits are to be split. A third kind of unincorporated body is a trust. If you want to start a charity to serve a particular community, this could be the right form for you (see p.135). Trusts can make up their own rules, but their social objectives are protected by a trust deed, which dictates how any assets can be used.

PROS AND CONS
Staying unincorporated

PROS

+ Less start-up bureaucracy

+ No need to complete annual returns and accounts

+ Tax/cash flow advantages

CONS

- Personally liable for business

- Harder to raise finance

- Not being taken seriously

- No formal structure

What's on the line?

Despite their differences, these forms share one defining characteristic: personal liability. In short, there is no legal or financial distinction between you (and your business partners) and the business. If the assets of your business aren't sufficient to cover any debts and liabilities, your personal assets – your home, your car, your savings – could be at risk.

Depending on your structure, this might affect your business in different ways. If you are thinking of starting up an ethical service with a friend or colleague, such as a recruitment company for conservation professionals, a partnership might allow you to pool your financial resources and skills. The downside is that you could be responsible if your partner can't pay their share of debts. Limited companies (see below) offer much greater protection for the individuals involved.

Companies have other advantages over sole traders and partnerships. Most loan managers or professional investors won't finance sole traders. Having a clear legal structure will also make it easier to purchase or rent property, and helps everyone – from your customers to your suppliers – take you and your ethical beliefs seriously.

If you are determined to drive the business forward, deciding to incorporate should be a question of when not if. Leading social enterprise law firm Bates, Wells & Braithwaite argue the following triggers may indicate it is time to incorporate:

- You plan to take on a lease
- You want to buy a freehold property
- You are looking to take on employees
- You want to raise finance
- You are entering into large contracts

Limited Liability Partnership

It is possible to combine some of the flexibility of being unincorporated with the protection of a private company. The **Limited Liability Partnership** (LLP) is a hybrid form, which is similar to a normal partnership but protects individuals against business debts. This structure was created mainly for professionals, such as lawyers and accountants, who wanted some form of limited liability.

If you are thinking of starting an eco-architecture practice, for example, this structure will give you the main benefit of incorporation – limited personal liability if the building you design falls down – without sacrificing the favourable tax treatment and organisational simplicity enjoyed by partnerships. While you won't have an official company constitution (see p.124), your ethical purpose can instead be written into your partnership agreement. In most other respects, LLPs face the same obligations as regular companies, and you will still have to prepare and file annual accounts.

Launching a company

More than one million small and medium-sized businesses in the UK are currently structured as private limited companies, rather than as sole traders or partnerships. One explanation is that setting up a company is incredibly easy. But perhaps more importantly, limited companies are separate legal entities. This means that if things go wrong, the people running them are not, typically, personally liable for company debts.

If you start a company that specialises in matching volunteers to particular charity projects, for example, any contracts that you enter into would be between your company, the individuals and charities only. Your personal assets are not at risk.

Protection

Limited liability is a huge selling point, but it's not a magic wand. It won't offer protection against investment loss, such as any personal savings you have already put into the business, and banks will often (though not always) require personal guarantees (e.g. your home) before awarding loans to start-ups and relatively young businesses. It might seem you're no better off than being a sole trader, except then, you would probably never have been offered the loan in the first place!

Nevertheless, having a formal company structure does make it easier to run a business. In theory, you have the flexibility to pay yourself what you like (even if in practice, cash and profit will restrict this). Company law also gives you a proper legal framework in which to grow, and the people you deal with are more likely to take you seriously if you have the paperwork to prove you are a professional outfit.

The basics

The Inland Revenue
www.hmrc.gov.uk

Government department to which companies pay direct taxes including income tax and national insurance contributions.

The are two main kinds of limited companies: companies limited by shares, and companies limited by guarantee. Their differences are outlined below. While each is easy to create, for both you will need to consider a number of ongoing administrative costs and obligations. As well as dealing with your own tax returns, you have to submit annual company accounts to Companies House and the Inland Revenue. You also need to submit annual returns, outlining any changes to the details of who owns and runs your company, and what it does. Depending on the size and nature of your company, there are other obligations too, including corporation tax and VAT. The Inland

Revenue website has detailed advice guides on what is required for your business.

Regular choice

The vast majority of companies are **Companies Limited by Shares** (CLS). The biggest benefit of this form is that you can raise capital through a private share issue. This has nothing to do with the stock exchange, where shares are traded publicly. Instead, this structure allows you to sell shares in your business directly to external shareholders. For start-ups, these are often the bosses and any friends, family or business partners you can convince to cough up. For most people, the idea of ploughing money into an unknown venture is an understandably risky proposition – so you may end up holding all the shares yourself. This may be no bad thing. Remember, each share is a percentage of your business. Retaining complete control may help you to grow the business the way you want to, and if your business is successful it will represent a great personal investment.

While a CLS is the structure of choice for most profit-making businesses, it is not an obviously distinct ethical form in the same way as a Community Interest Company (see p.126). The common assumption will be that your objectives are purely financial, which means you may have to work extra hard to convince people that you are running an ethical enterprise.

Setting up a CLS means choosing a level playing field among the competition; you get all the flexibility and freedom of a regular share-issuing company, but none of the perks of a less profit-oriented structure (many grant-awarding bodies won't accept applications from a CLS). This might sound counter-productive, but

PROS AND CONS
Company Limited by Shares

PROS

+ Limited personal liability

+ Separate legal entity

+ Democratic structure

+ Can also be a CIC
  (see p.126)

+ Access to share finance

CONS

- No clear ethical
  kitemark (other than
  Memorandum and
  Articles of Association)

- Responsible to
  shareholders

- Difficult to get
  grant funding

ethical credentials alone are not a guarantee of business success. Generating growth finance through trading, persuading investors of your trustworthiness and out-performing your competitors is often the most reliable route to success. The CLS is the route that the three founders of Innocent Drinks took when they started up. Today, they run the biggest smoothie brand in the UK, and the company is regarded as an ethical pioneer.

The ethical angle

There are also ways to ensure the structure of your CLS explicitly addresses social, environmental and other ethical considerations. Any company that offers shares as part of its structure can give "golden share" agreements to individuals or organisations, which gives them special control over the business. If you decide to set up a packing company staffed by people with learning difficulties, you could give the employees and their families a golden share. Because they part-own the company, they can ensure the core values of the business remain in their interests, which for your staff are likely to be more than merely financial.

Perhaps the most direct way to safeguard your core ethical principles, however, is to write them directly into your company's constitution (see p.124). Your constitution governs how your business operates on a day-to-day basis.

Price to pay

There is a price to pay with any share-issuing structure. Your shareholders effectively buy an investment in your business, and will usually expect clear financial returns from it. Should they be unhappy, or an external party buys up a majority stake in your business, they could force out the existing management team. That might mean you.

Perhaps the highest profile case of an ethical takeover involved The Body Shop. In March 2006, it was bought out by French cosmetics giant L'Oréal in a deal worth £652 million. Even though The Body Shop retained its core values, many people felt disappointed that one of Britain's pioneer ethical businesses had been swallowed up by a global corporation.

A "golden share" or alternative anti-takeover share arrangement may not have allowed that scenario to happen, as Helen Ireland, head of corporate communications at the UK's largest fair trade hot drinks company Cafédirect, explained.

WHY WE BECAME... A Company Limited by Shares

 Red Ochre is a specialist business support consultancy to the voluntary and social enterprise sector, run by director Uday Thakkar.

A lot of so-called social enterprises (see p.112) won't do anything unless they get grant funding. In other words, they won't take risks. Grant reliance also affects strategy and leads to vision drift. Partly because I object to that mentality, Red Ochre is set up as a company limited by shares. We can't get grants even if we wanted to. We've purposely done it to show we don't need the grants – that we're going to go out and do what we do and prove we do it well. We want to rely purely on ourselves rather than the ability to pull in grants.

Being a CLS requires a personal financial commitment and wonderfully concentrates the mind. Decision-making is swift and consensus quickly achieved. The requirement for delivering multiple outcomes – social, environmental and financial – is challenging enough without having to work with a stakeholder group on your board who may have diverse agendas. Transparency and governance best practice follow the values of the management and not the legal structure.

www.redochre.org.uk

"At Cafédirect we couldn't be taken over in the same way. We made a conscious decision two years ago when the articles were put together that funders would take a guardian share that would protect the company's ethics and prohibit a takeover," she told New Consumer magazine.

"Recently we did a public share issue raising £5 million in less than four months through a sticker advertising shares on our packs. Rather than ownership by a faceless brand, our shareholders are precisely our buyers: individuals who believe in our ethos and a financial and social return."

Charity business

The other kind of company structure is heavily geared towards charitable enterprise. Owners, or "members" of **Companies Limited by Guarantee** (CLG) cannot draw any profit from the business, and are not allowed to raise money through shares.

Like a CLS, this form still has the protection of limited liability. Members generally promise to pay a nominal sum – usually £1 – in the event of the company being wound up. The members elect, and remove, a board of directors, who take care of the day-to-day running of the company. The key difference is that any surpluses made by a CLG are ploughed back into the business. A salary is the only thing you can take out of the company.

Many charities are set up as CLGs. It is an effective way to run a business, and every penny of profit goes back into the organisation's core work. But the advent of Community Interest Companies (see p.126) – which limit profit distribution and have a strong capacity for entrepreneurship – could see their popularity diminish.

PROS AND CONS
Company Limited by Guarantee

PROS

+ Limited personal liability

+ Separate legal entity

+ Greater access to grant funding

+ Not responsible to shareholders

CONS

- 100 per cent non-profit distributing

- Less reward for owners

- Cannot raise capital through shareholders

Not all CLGs are charities, however. If you start a consultancy to help local councils reduce waste, you may simply want to guarantee that all your profits go back into the business. One big advantage is that – as a clearly non-profit distributing structure – you may be eligible for certain grants and preferential loans (see Chapter 9: Raising Finance).

Getting started

Despite a certain amount of scaremongering by specialist websites who want to help (and charge) to set up a company for you, the DIY approach is fast and relatively straightforward. This will leave you more time and money to concentrate on getting

WHY WE BECAME... A Company Limited by Guarantee

 Climate Care is a non-profit distributing company which enables businesses and individuals to offset their carbon emissions.

The company chose this structure to prevent any conflict of interest between its mission of reducing greenhouse gases in the atmosphere and its commercial goals.

A company limited by shares has an overarching purpose to make money for its shareholders. A company limited by guarantee has no shareholders. So there is no conflict between shareholders' interests and the company's stated mission.

Climate Care Trust Ltd has a royalty relationship which is open and transparent. It pays a capped royalty of 10 per cent of turnover to Climate Care Ltd – a separate company that has provided the Trust with financial and management resources over the years.

There are some minor disadvantages to not being a PLC – it can be more difficult to access capital markets and there are some commercial restrictions – but these are not severe."

www.climatecare.co.uk

the ethos of your company right. Simply order a free starter park from Companies House. Return this and a cheque for the registration fee (£20 at time of press), and you could have a brand new company in four days. There is even a same-day service (currently £50). You will need to complete and send off a total of four forms.

- Form No. 10 requires details of the registered office and who will be running the company; here, you need to specify a "director" and a "company secretary". If you are the sole director, you cannot also be company secretary.

- Form No. 12 is a declaration that you will abide by the Companies Act.

- The other two documents are your Articles of Association and Memorandum. Together, these form your company's constitution and are a golden opportunity to set in stone the ethical values that underscore your entire business.

Writing an ethical constitution

What is the core purpose of your business? How will you distribute any profits? What rights do you as company director hold? The answers to these and many more questions will be found in your company's constitution, outlined in your Memorandum and Articles of Association.

The **Memorandum** sets out the name and location of your company, and what it aims to do in relation to the outside world. For many start-ups, this needs no further explanation than "being a commercial business". As an ethical business, however, you have an opportunity here to define exactly what makes your company socially and environmentally responsible. If you run a fair trade food shop, but are thinking about branching out into catering as well, make sure that your description is broad enough to take in this and any other future diversification. Remember, your company can only lawfully trade within the scope of this document.

The **Articles of Association** regulate the internal workings of your business. In other words, they set out the rules for all company affairs and management, such as the procedures for meetings and dividend entitlements to shareholders. As an ethical business, this is where you can write your values clearly into the heart of your company structure. If you are an environmentally conscious web design consultancy, you could have a zero air miles company policy, as well as a commitment to publish an annual environmental report on your business impacts.

Sets of model Memorandum and Articles of Association documents can be purchased from any legal stationers or formation agent for around £20-£30; and you can amend and add to them as you wish. You will also find sample Memorandums and Articles of Association for every kind of

All change?

The precise legal framework of a company's constitution – along with several other things relating to company law – will be revised when the Companies Act 2006 comes into force. The Act – intended to simplify existing law – had already received Royal Assent as this book went to press, but still requires additional secondary legislation. Most provisions of the Act are expected to come into force by October 2008. Visit the Department for Trade and Industry (DTI) website and Companies House for the latest developments.

incorporated structure on the internet. If you're thinking about setting up a charity, you might refer to the Governance Hub's constitutional code and the Charity Commission for guidance.

If you're a social enterprise, you can find a set of model rules for several different legal structures on the Social Enterprise Coalition website. This can help you with the wording and highlight any areas you may have missed. The Co-operatives UK website also has model rules for different co-operatives (see p.129), while the Community Interest Company Regulator homepage has free, downloadable model constitutions for different kinds of CICs (see below). Since your constitution is critical to your everyday ethical actions, you might also consider getting a legal specialist to look over your final draft version.

Governance Hub
www.governancehub.org.uk

Offers a set of principles for charities and voluntary organisations explaining the roles of the board and trustees and ensuring a high standard of governance.

Co-operatives UK
www.cooperatives-uk.coop

Umbrella body and forum, which aims to raise awareness of and provide a voice for large and small co-operative enterprises in the UK.

Community Interest Companies Regulator
www.cicregulator.gov.uk

Government organisation, which registers businesses as CICs if they meet certain community benefiting criteria.

Community Interest Companies: Another Way

A new legal structure has been set up specifically for ethical business. **Community Interest Companies** (CICs – pronounced "kicks") are designed to create both profit and community benefit. They are often dubbed the halfway house between charities and companies.

Like private companies, CICs can be limited by guarantee or shares. What stops them being purely commercial is something called an "Asset Lock". This is an inbuilt control that limits the amount of money that can be taken out of the business. You, as the director, (and any shareholders) can only take a limited amount of the company's profits. As a rough guide, two thirds of profits must be ploughed back into the business (or to another asset-locked CIC or charity); only around one third can be paid out as dividends. Being a CIC sends out a clear message that the company's values, rather than shareholder profit, are at the heart of your business.

While this has some obvious similarities with the CLG structure, share-issuing CICs are arguably more entrepreneurial creatures. The ability to raise finance through shares, and be rewarded if the business succeeds, provides a great incentive for future growth.

Advantages

One of the biggest upsides to the CIC form is access to finance. If you decide to start an organic meals-on-wheels service as a CIC, your legal structure will have a clear community benefit and may enable you to apply for several grants and special favourable loans that are not open to regular companies. You will, however, still have to pay the same taxes as everyone else; only charities receive tax relief.

With more and more companies looking to jump on the ethical bandwagon, CICs are also a very effective way to prove your ethical credentials. After all, not everyone can be a CIC. To qualify, you have to present a written report (known as the "Community Interest Statement") explaining how your business will actively benefit the community, and this has to pass a "Community Interest Test". Once approved, you have to file an extra annual report with your accounts to show how the business has lived up to these expectations.

PROS AND CONS
Community Interest Company

PROS

+ Clearly ethical business
+ Limited personal liability
+ Separate legal entity
+ Access to more funding streams

CONS

- Relatively unknown legal form
- Restricted use of company money
- No special tax breaks

Drawbacks

As with any new legal form, a major drawback is lack of recognition. CICs are still relatively unknown and you may need to explain the concept to confused bank managers or convince grant-making bodies that you are actually allowed to apply for their funding.

Another downside is that CICs may be too restrictive for many entrepreneurs. While directors can earn good money through salaries, if you set up and grow a business for 30 years, you might also expect to be rewarded at the end of it. The Asset Lock prevents this. If a CIC is wound up, its assets are reserved for the community. This undoubtedly displays a strong commitment to

WHY WE BECAME... A Community Interest Company

 Striding Out is an award-winning support network for young entrepreneurs. Its director is Heather Wilkinson.

I wanted Striding Out to be a rapidly innovating organisation, and also wanted to retain control and direction over our services. The CIC model seemed ideal. Having a charitable status and establishing a trustee board would have meant losing an element of this entrepreneurial dynamism, whilst employee-ownership models (e.g. co-operatives) were unsuitable for me based on my sole directorship. Nevertheless, I still wanted to instil confidence in our funders, clients and stakeholders that we would reinvest our income back into supporting our beneficiaries, rather than retain them for any private profit.

The CIC model has achieved this, and we have successfully secured grants from a number of organisations. Unlike a charity, we cannot access any tax relief and tapping into corporate sponsors can prove difficult, so there are a few constraints. But it is important for social businesses to be commercially viable. Having the CIC status installs this entrepreneurial mindset and culture within Striding Out, and draws us away from slipping into grant dependency.

www.stridingout.co.uk

ethical values, but many entrepreneurial minds might be deterred by the potential financial sacrifice.

IPS: Society works

Unlike limited companies, **Industrial and Provident Societies** (IPS) are organisational structures specifically designed to benefit a particular community. There are two kinds of IPS:

■ **Co-operatives** – run to benefit their members
■ **Community Benefit Societies** (BenComs) – run to benefit the wider community

Unlike a company limited by guarantee, an IPS can typically raise regular share capital. Rather unusually, it can also issue "withdrawable shares" which can be bought back from shareholders at a later stage. This enables you to access share finance without risking losing of control of the business.

When the Phone Co-op, an ethical, customer-owned telecommunications business, switched from being a company limited by guarantee to an IPS, it raised money for future growth through just such a withdrawable share issue. Today, its annual turnover exceeds £4 million.

Co-operatives

If you want to start a business, being a boss isn't the only option. Rigid concepts of management are not only restrictive for those at the bottom of the ladder, they can also be hugely inefficient. Employees on the factory floor, for example, are often the first to identify emerging problems and new opportunities.

But in many companies, their voices are rarely heard.

Co-operatives aim to create a much more democratic and productive working environment. The most famous example of a co-op in Britain is, yes, The Co-op. Its supermarket and bank are household names, but The Co-operative Group also owns travel agencies, shoe shops, pharmacies, a farming management business and even funeral parlours. Despite their obvious differences, each business is based on the long-standing traditions of the global co-operative movement. At its core, this means each business is owned and run by its members, rather than by a single owner creaming off the profits. Each aims to contribute to the "well-being and enrichment of society" by re-investing profits into the business and local communities. Co-ops also come in all shapes and sizes; you can set one up as a partnership, a company limited by shares or guarantee, or as a CIC. But the majority are registered as an IPS.

Regardless of legal structure, every co-operative shares the following core values:

- Voluntary and open membership
- Democratic member control
- Economic participation by members
- Autonomy and independence
- Education, training and information for members and employees
- Working with other co-operatives
- Concern for the community

Rich heritage

As you might expect from a movement steeped in history, there are many different kinds of co-operatives. Here are some of the most common types:

Consumers' co-operatives: e.g. a local food shop. Consumer co-ops are owned by the people who buy the goods or use their services.

Workers' co-operatives: e.g. a printers. Workers co-ops are owned and controlled by the people who work in them. They also share the responsibilities and rewards of the business.

Community co-operatives: e.g. a local recycling service. Community co-ops are owned and controlled by people in the community.

Service or marketing co-operatives: e.g. dairy farmers. Marketing co-ops enable small businesses to pool their resources to take on very large jobs.

Housing co-operatives: provide housing for their members, and are controlled by the people who live in them.

Food co-operatives: enable people to buy cheaper, better quality food by using their purchasing power to buy from wholesalers or in bulk.

Highs and lows

If you want to create a company rooted in equality, the co-op structure gives you a ready-made template. This is the way that Leeds-based printers Footprint functions. A workers' co-operative, it was set up in July 2000 to provide printing services to the highest possible ethical and environmental standards. Membership is offered to all trained workers (currently three part-time members, each working about 15 hours a week). All members are directors of the company and receive the same rate of pay.

Depending on how you set up your co-op, the business itself is run either by an elected board of directors (a group of members democratically elected each year) or by all the members actively participating in decision-making. The downside of including everyone is that it can take a long time to agree on the big decisions. Indeed, some co-ops take so long in their consultations that they risk never getting anything done.

If you are starting a co-operative from scratch, there is also a risk that the common bond shared by the initial members will become diluted as more and more people join the business. Since everyone has an equal say, new people could arrive and change your direction. Nevertheless, if everyone is pulling the

WHY WE BECAME... A Co-operative

 Health food wholesaler Suma is the one of the UK's largest 100 per cent worker-owned co-operatives. Andrew Mackintosh is a co-operative member.

One of the best things about being a co-op is transparency. Everybody here knows the strengths and weaknesses of the business. There are no underlings telling the bosses what they want to hear. The fact that everyone here can do at least three other jobs also means they can slot into somebody else's role if they're sick.

This flexibility is a really efficient way to work.

There is an incredible sense of trust and camaraderie, which I've never experienced elsewhere. Yes, the decision-making process can be ponderous, but it has got better.

In addition, every level of our supply chain is governed by our company ethics. The workers own

and control the business and because we are all directors, we are all paid the same, whatever our role. Currently, that's £30,000 plus benefits, which is very good for a distribution company and well above the national average.

www.suma.co.uk

same way, the co-operative structure can be a highly flexible, effective and fair way to work.

BenComs

The other kind of IPS is the Community Benefit Society, aka the BenCom. As the name suggests, the chief purpose is to ensure that your community (and not just your members) benefit from your ethical business. If you are planning to start a nursery school in a disadvantaged area, you could use this form to let your staff take part in decision-making, while fixing in stone your social objectives to the local community.

They key point here is that (unlike with co-ops) all profits must be earmarked for the wider community, not for your members or any external shareholders. Also unlike co-ops, BenComs can apply for charitable status. As a charitable BenCom, you could raise capital through public grants and charitable trusts, and would be eligible for Gift Aid (tax relief on donations to your charity).

The basics

BenComs and co-ops registered as IPS are regulated not by Companies House, but by the Financial Services Authority (FSA). The reporting obligations are less stringent, but you still need to submit annual accounts.

While almost anyone can become a member of (and buy up shares in) an IPS, an interesting feature of all co-operatives and most BenComs is the "one member, one vote" system. In limited companies, the number of shares held decides the strength of your voting power. People with 5,000 shares therefore

PROS AND CONS
Industrial and Provident Society (Co-op & BenCom)

PROS

+ Clearly ethical business

+ Limited liability

+ Truly democratic

+ Common sense of ownership

CONS

- Expensive and relatively complex to register

- Slow decision making

- Less personal control

- Less familiar to many banks

Financial Services Authority
www.fsa.gov.uk

An independent body, accountable to Treasury ministers, that regulates the financial services industry in the UK.

Disability first

More than 80 per cent of people in the UK with learning difficulties do not currently have a paid job. This alienation from the workforce can have a profoundly negative effect on those who desperately do want to work. In mainstream business, there are often misconceptions that disabled people cannot fulfil a useful function, or will need lots of extra care or specialised equipment. Innovative, flexible enterprises recognise that this is not always the case. **Social firms** are businesses specifically set up to create employment for people with mental or physical disabilities. They are not a legal form, but adhere to three overriding principles: enterprise, employment and empowerment.

According to Social Firms UK, more than 25 per cent of any social firm's employees should be disabled. But they're not just there to make up the numbers. Social firms pay all employees the same as, or above, the national average, and are "equal and fair" in their treatment of all employees, regardless of disability. They also aim to earn at least half of their turnover through sales of goods or services. In other words, they try not to be grant dependent. Some social firms which employ people with complex learning disabilities may need to consider support services very seriously. Other businesses employing workers with less complex disabilities may find they need very little disability-specific services at all.

If you are thinking about starting a business that requires a diverse range of skill sets, being a social firm could be a powerful way to put some of your ethical values at the heart of the business. That's what Pack-IT Product Promotions Limited has achieved in almost 20 years of trading. Originally set up to provide training opportunities and paid employment for people with learning disabilities, it began as a small, light industrial packing service. Today, it employs more than 20 full-time staff, half of whom have Down's Syndrome, are profoundly deaf or have behavioural and learning difficulties.

The company's strong social goals haven't weakened its financial performance. Between 1994 and 2003, Pack-IT's turnover increased from £70,000 to £1.2 million. All accrued profits (currently £121,000) are ploughed back into the business, invested in people and machinery. If you have the same ambition and commitment to providing long-term employment for disadvantaged people, there is nothing to stop you enjoying the same success.

have a much greater say than people with five. But an IPS allocates one vote to every member, regardless of how many shares they own. The members effectively manage the organisation.

One drawback of registering an IPS is the cost. To register, you need a set of "rules", the equivalent of your constitution. If you create yours from scratch, it will cost £950 and you will likely need legal help to write them. Alternatively, you can buy a set of model rules from the FSA for £40 although any changes to them will incur further costs. As always, it is worth asking a legal advisor to check over your amendments.

Social Firms UK
www.socialfirms.co.uk

Umbrella body which aims to create employment opportunities for disabled people through the development and support of social enterprises.

Charities

There are currently more than 160,000 charities registered in England and Wales, and yet more in Scotland and Northern Ireland. Together, they work to alleviate a myriad of social and environmental problems: from their local communities to the poorest nations in the world. If your business idea also involves helping a group of people or the planet, you may share some similarities with a charity. But that doesn't mean you can automatically join the club. To become eligible as a charity, you need to prove that your organisation meets three key criteria:

1. It is for public benefit

2. It has exclusively charitable aims

3. It is actively involved in one of the following areas:

- the prevention or relief of poverty
- the advancement of education, religion or animal welfare
- the advancement of health or the saving of lives

- the advancement of citizenship or community development
- the advancement of the arts, culture, heritage or science
- the advancement of amateur sport
- the advancement of human rights, conflict resolution or reconciliation or the promotion of religious or racial harmony or equality and diversity
- the advancement of environmental protection or improvement
- the relief of those in need by reason of youth, age, ill health, disability, financial hardship or other disadvantage
- the promotion of the efficiency of the armed forces of the Crown; or the efficiency of the police, fire and rescue services or ambulance services

A key theme here is wider public benefit. You can't set up a charity to help your friend pay for his university studies, even if that does sound rather like "the advancement of education".

The basics

What unites all charities is non-profit distribution. This means that any surpluses made cannot be paid out; they must be ploughed back into the organisation. If you want the freedom to use profits how you want, being a charity is not for you.

There are other financial limitations too. As a charity, your directors (usually called trustees) are responsible for the administration and management of the organisation, but they are also typically unpaid. As a result, if you found a charity – and want to earn a wage for your work – you will most likely not serve on the board of trustees. This is problematic if you also want to control the ultimate direction of the organisation.

Historically, if you were looking to start a charity with all the benefits of limited personal liability, you had to register as a charity with the Charity Commission and as a company with Companies House. Under the Charities Act 2006, all this is set to change. The Act creates a new legal structure, known, rather logically, as a Charitable Incorporated Organisation. This will give trustees limited liability without the burden of dual registration.

At the time of print, more legislation is required for this new structure to take full effect. Keep an eye on the Charity Commission's website for all the latest developments. This website also has numerous resources to help you register as a charity, including model constitution documents and a downloadable application pack. To register, you will need to send in:

- A completed application form
- Your constitution
- CVs of the initial board members
- An initial business plan
- A set of standard forms (available from the Charity Commission) signed by each trustee to say they are aware of their responsibilities.

Depending on the length and complexity of your application, the registration process can take anything from a few weeks to several months.

Charity Commission
www.charity-commission.gov.uk

Organisation responsible for registering charities in England and Wales, which keeps online copies of a charity's accounts.

Benefits

If you meet the criteria, there are several reasons for wanting to be a charity. One is simply a question of perception. If you start a marine conservation project as a charity, you may be perceived differently than the same operation registered only as a company. For many people, charities are seen as intrinsically ethical organisations. Rightly or wrongly, just by having the words "Registered Charity" on your website and letterhead, you will be deemed a worthy cause. This can help if you need to raise funds for a particular project.

There is another financial incentive too. As well as benefiting from public fundraising, if you set up a charity you could also tap into considerable amounts of funding from the numerous grant-awarding bodies in the UK and beyond (see p.167).

Charities also enjoy extremely generous tax benefits. They are exempt from income/corporation tax, capital gains tax and stamp duties. They also receive at least 80 per cent exemption from business rates on premises, and may also receive Gift Aid – where the government contributes another 28p for every £1 raised by your charity from UK taxpayers. These are the reasons that many social enterprises seek charitable status.

Drawbacks

Despite this apparent monetary windfall, insufficient finance remains most charities' number one headache. Relying on public generosity and winning grants is unpredictable at best. As a result, your enterprise's financial health could vary wildly from year to year, and this can have serious effects on your goals. Lack of long-term capital can mean good works are begun, only to be left incomplete.

Charities also have rather complex issues of ownership, more typically called "governance". If you decide to start a charity, you will need to find other people to sit on a board of trustees. These people are unpaid, but they will collectively decide on the organisation's strategic direction. If you and any other paid employees have other ideas for the charity, this can be a frustrating experience. Furthermore, without one single person in charge – and with no financial incentive for any of the decision-makers – it's easy to see how decisions can take a long time and not be especially business-focused.

Other downsides to the charity route include the complex registration procedures and heavy regulation by the Charity Commission (although the new Act promises to alleviate bureaucracy). Currently, charities with an annual income of more than £10,000 have to file annual reports, accounts and an annual return, which are subject to considerable scrutiny by the Charity Commission.

Trading charities

Being a charity does not mean you always have to sit back and ask for money. Charities are also allowed to earn funds from providing goods and services. There are, however, limitations on the kind of business you can undertake.

As a charity, you can normally only trade in your primary purpose, i.e. what you're set up to do. An animal shelter could not, for example, start selling something entirely unrelated – such as garden furniture – to finance its good work. Consequently,

WHY WE BECAME... A Trading Charity

A Change of AdDress is an innovative new charity shop in North London, aimed at helping women former offenders.

Like most charity executive directors, Jocelyn Hillman had spent many sleepless nights thinking about new ways to raise money. Her charity, Dress For Success, helps disadvantaged women get back to work by providing them with smart clothes. When a woman leaves prison, for example, she may have nothing appropriate to wear for a job interview.

Dress For Success gives them the right outfit and accessories to make a good impression. It also goes through different role play scenarios and interview techniques to help boost self-esteem and confidence. For many women, it's an invaluable helping hand back into society. Since the charity started up six years ago, it had been giving away surplus clothes to other local charities. But after spending more time with women offenders in London's Holloway Prison in the summer of 2006, Jocelyn came up with a more entrepreneurial solution. In partnership with the prison, she decided to open a very different kind of charity shop.

'A Change of AdDress' will be staffed by former offenders who receive on-the-job retail training from qualified trainers; at the end of it, they will receive an NVQ Stage 2 qualification. Women on day release will be able to come in and work before the end of their sentences. The charity has also created ties with the local job centre to help the women move on to the next stage of employment. As well as clothes, the shop will also sell crafts made by the women in Holloway Prison. There are also plans for a tailoring and repair service. The shop's twin aims are to increase the charity's revenue stream and enhance its impact. Ultimately, Jocelyn would like to see some of the ex-offenders represented on the charity's board of trustees. As a Company Limited by Guarantee, it is currently looking for grant funding to cover the shop's start-up costs. But the clear goal is to reduce the charity's current reliance on donations.

"Within three years, I'm hopeful we can be self-financing," says Jocelyn. "Then we could start rolling out the idea to other prisons."

many charities set up a separate trading company, which is owned by the charity and contributes its profits to it. This is a perfectly legal workaround.

An advantage of setting up a for-profit business in this way – usually as a company limited by shares, but also as a CIC – is that it has separate limited liability. If the business arm fails, it won't bring down the charity. This is how marine conservation charity Blue Ventures Conservation works. It runs a for-profit marine expedition business which gives all of its profits back to the main charity.

But as a trading charity, you will need to perform a careful balancing act. Employee bonus schemes, for example, might serve a useful purpose in a regular company. But as a charity, you have an overriding obligation to the "public benefit". Some financial incentives for staff might conflict with this, and you need to make sure that you don't compromise the charity's objectives. Depending on your choice of business, there could be other potential conflicts. If you're thinking about setting up a trading company, it's a good idea to read the "Charities and Trading" publication on the Charity Commission website and seek advice from a specialist charity lawyer.

9 Raising Finance

IN THIS CHAPTER...

- How to find start-up capital
- Where to source ethical finance
- How to get finance-ready
- Where to look for different funding

NO MATTER HOW great your idea, your business cannot survive without sufficient capital – the cash behind your company that gets it off the ground. The good news is that there are literally dozens of different ways to raise the money you need to support your early growth. The bad news? Let's just say young businesses aren't exactly top of a bank manager's dream client list. As for young ethical businesses, trying to explain your social and environmental values to a high-street lender, who is interested only in your profit forecasts, could be a pretty uninspiring experience.

But for all the ignorance and misunderstanding still prevalent among some mainstream banks, the tide is turning. Awareness not only of sustainable business as a concept, but as a profitable business model, is growing. If you can show that your company will also deliver solid financial returns, you will make an impressive case for finance. If the banks still don't want to know, remember that loans are not the only options out there.

If you need to raise money for your business, you have three main options:

- **Equity** is finance given in return for a stake in the business. If you are a limited company, this will be in the form of shares.

- **Debt** is money borrowed from a lender; the most common forms are bank loans and overdrafts.

- **Grants** are financial awards that do not have to be repaid. Grants are a main source of finance for many charities, but other kinds of sustainable business may also be eligible.

If you need money to finance your new ethical company, your choice of capital may not simply pay for the start-up phase; it can also affect how you operate the business on a daily basis. Equity, debt and grants typically come with different strings attached, which may (or may not) suit your ethics, or push your business in a certain direction. In this chapter, we will be looking at all of these issues.

For many new enterprises, it's not capital but cash flow – the availability of money at any given time – which causes the biggest headache. It is no use if your business is solvent on paper, for example, if you get paid several months after you need to pay your suppliers.

The right mix

Your ideal mix of finance will depend on this and other factors. How much money you require will depend on the kind of business you are looking to start, for example whether you need to buy any expensive equipment. It also depends on your mindset. Do you have any assets that you could put up as a guarantee against a loan? Are you prepared to do that? Would you be prepared to remortgage a home? How much personal risk are you willing to take on?

When you're planning a business geared towards achieving much more than just profit, focusing on money is perhaps the last thing you want to do. But the financial performance of your enterprise will make or break the business and this will determine what kind of impact you can achieve. Great intentions need rock solid finances.

Friends and family

You may be too old for pocket money, but family and friends are a good first port of call for start-up funding. If you can convince them of the greater good of your ethical idea, they may just be willing to help out. Many successful entrepreneurs raised the cash they needed to get their first solo idea off the ground from family. There are obvious advantages to this route. Families are less likely than a bank to scrutinise your business plan, expect much lower returns, and, crucially, are much more disposed to saying yes. Naturally, if you have any personal savings to contribute, dig deep before asking others.

For many businesses under 12-months old, don't be alarmed if this is the only source of debt or equity finance you can access. It is sad, but predictable, that mainstream lenders will typically back an experienced business head with an average idea over a first-timer with a sure-fire winner – even if your idea is going to make the world a better place. Don't take it personally. Try to be creative with what you have at your disposal, and remember that if you can show healthy sets of books after the first few years, you will become a much more attractive proposition.

Revenue

If you want to start a socially responsible website design company, and don't need a lot of capital to start up, going after sales might be the best way to get money into your business. Chasing banks and other funders can take a long time, and if you don't need the investment right now, there is nothing to stop you from trading. Besides the extra money, getting orders can also be a great confidence booster. If you want to break into it gently, you could plan a test phase with a select group of consumers a few months before you go live. This "soft launch" is a good way to see how thing work in practice – and to iron out any glitches – before you officially open for business.

For Elaine James at ethical public relations company Koan, the revenue approach gave her a sense of security and peace of mind. "For me, being debt free was really important. It can be difficult to achieve, but it gives you a lot more freedom."

Loans

If you do need finance to start up, loans are one solution. Happily, as an ethical business, you will have many more options here than solely profit-orientated companies. Besides the usual run of high-street banks, there are a number of lenders aimed specifically at enterprises with strong social and environmental policies.

Choosing an ethical lender might also fit better with your principles. If you are concerned about the corporate behaviour of a high-street bank, you may prefer to deal only with more ethical lenders (see p.150).

Early issues

Even if you do approach the high-street banks, you may find them reluctant to lend to your business. After all, start-ups are a risky investment and if profit isn't your only motivation, you may have a tough job persuading them to part with their cash. Even if you do, they will often demand a personal guarantee, such as your home.

If you're already incorporated, being asked for a guarantee seems particularly harsh. After all, one of the reasons for setting up a company is to protect your personal liability. But if the bank deems you a risky bet, they can be impossible to avoid. Nevertheless, think carefully before putting your personal assets on the line, and don't be afraid to shop around with different lenders to see if any are prepared to drop the guarantee or come to a compromise. If you have a lot of expensive stock, for example, the bank may be prepared to use that as an alternative security. If you

No strings attached?

The Small Firms Loan Guarantee (SFLG) is a scheme aimed at start-ups and young businesses who find it difficult to raise enough finance.

As a new ethical business, you may face just this problem. If your idea is considered too risky or you don't have a strong business track record, for example, you may not get very far with the banks unless you can offer a sizeable personal guarantee.

With the SFLG, banks still get a guarantee, but it's the government, not you, who will ease their worried minds. In return, they will happily provide you a loan. The government guarantee covers 75 per cent of the loan, which can range from £5,000 to £250,000 for between two and 10 years. (You may have to give a personal guarantee for the remaining 25 per cent.)

To qualify, your business must be under five years old and have a turnover of less than £5.6 million. In return for the guarantee, you pay the Department of Trade and Industry (DTI) a premium of 2 per cent per year on the outstanding amount of the loan.

have nothing of value to offer, the Small Firms Loan Guarantee could be the answer.

Catch 22

If you're setting up in business with someone else, personal guarantees can have added implications. When Tom Pakenham and Jonny Goldstone of low emission taxi firm Green Tomato Cars took out vehicle finance to buy their initial fleet, one director had a house and family, while the other didn't. They got the money they needed, but only after both had given personal guarantees, which affected them in very different ways.

"It's a Catch 22," says Tom. "If you're young and you have no assets, the banks won't give you a loan.

If you're older and have a house and family, it's very stressful to risk everything. For about a month, I was basically a wreck. I didn't sleep well and was losing a lot of weight. I was very nervous the whole time. Since then, we've made it a company policy not to give any more personal guarantees."

"It also had an impact on our relationship," says Jonny. "We are sharing the burden equally, but I've got a lot less to lose. So Tom was going through stress that I didn't have."

Guarantees can also be thorny issues if your legal form is more geared to charity enterprise. If you start a café staffed by people with learning disabilities as a company limited by guarantee, you can't take any profit out of the business. Given this, would you want to put up your house as the security on a loan? Not wanting to take this kind of personal risk is the reason that many trading charities find themselves caught in the grant trap (see p.166).

There are many different kinds of loan; from regular fixed-term agreements and loans specifically for buying property or equipment, through to bridging

Tip... Check your credit

★ Before you get in touch with any lender, order a copy of your **credit report**. This is a record of your personal credit history, which the bank will use when judging any loan application.

You can order this very cheaply from a number of companies (Experian and Equifax are two of the most popular) and check there are no blemishes on your record. One late payment or a clerical error, for example,

could damage your credit status and affect your chances of being approved. If you spot these in advance, you can resolve any problems before applying for a loan or overdraft.

loans, which can help resolve cash-flow problems. Before calling the bank, determine what product you need and then shop around. The Money Supermarket website is a great place to start. Once you know what you want, remember to always take your time to check through any small print, and never deal with an unauthorised lender.

High-street banks

Mainstream banks are getting better at recognising and understanding ethical business. Natwest/RBS, for example, has a special department that considers applications from social enterprises. But your local branch may well be unaware of its existence. Instead, go to the bank's website and search for "Community Development Banking".

As an ethical business, though, you may want to consider whether to deal with high-street banks at all. Some well-known lenders have very poor records on human rights. If you have strong feelings about this, you may not want to support an institution which finances the sales of arms or offers inappropriate amounts of credit to vulnerable people who are already in debt. Ultimately, this will be a personal decision. As we have seen (see p.59) there are a number of more ethical options when it comes to opening a bank account. The same is true for loan finance, and we will consider these later in this chapter.

If you do decide to venture onto the high street, be warned that most loan managers won't look beyond your profit forecast and business background. According to a 2006 survey by Venture Finance, 75 per cent of companies feel that mainstream banks lack the vision needed to work with ethical entrepreneurs

Money Supermarket
www.moneysupermarket.com

An independent online price comparison site, which provides information on the best deals on everything from personal loans to insurance.

"who run their businesses without damaging the environment, exploiting workforces or producing harmful products". If you start an ethical technology company, and want to show how your financial and your social goals combine to create a business that can compete in the IT industry, this can prove a very frustrating experience.

Ethical lenders

Some banks are specifically geared to ethical business. Their loans managers know all about triple bottom lines and actively discriminate in favour of this kind of enterprise. You may also feel more comfortable about borrowing from a lender which doesn't deal with unethical businesses and that is committed to positive social change. While these "social banks" will be much more aligned with your ethical values, however, they will still want the same level of security expected by a regular lender.

For David Lamb, loans manager at social bank Triodos, a lack of adequate financial preparation is often the biggest hurdle for ethical entrepreneurs. "Quite often you meet people who have a wonderful idea that is close to their hearts. But in many respects the idea takes over from reality. They haven't really thought if it is viable."

All banks have similar criteria when it comes to assessing risk. First, they look at your business plan. This needs to be succinct, hard-hitting and credible. Regardless of your ethical motivations, it has to convince experienced loans managers that you have a financially viable business and a realistic cash flow forecast; in other words, that you will be in a position to repay the debt. If they are impressed, they will then look at the people running the enterprise. Do you have experience in this sector? What is your loan history? A strong track record counts for a lot, but there are other ways to make a good impression too.

When eco-clothing company Howies approached Triodos for a loan, it was a last ditch attempt to raise vital capital. Founder David Hieatt admits that the numbers "never quite added up", but was counting on his team making a better impression than their business plan.

"The guy at Triodos stuck his neck out where most people wouldn't. Purely on a banking decision, they shouldn't have accepted us. But I said, 'Look round the table. Do you have the confidence we can do it?' And he decided to back us."

Triodos Bank
www.triodos.co.uk

Ethical bank, which uses investors' money to finance companies, institutions and projects that add "cultural value" and benefit people and the environment.

JARGON BUSTING... Sweat equity

Benjamin Franklin first coined the expression "Time is money". Sadly, this won't mean much for most new entrepreneurs. When it comes to setting up a business, you may be putting in a huge amount of your time for very little financial reward. This unpaid toil is known as "sweat equity". If it is your business, you may simply have to write this off as the cost of laying the right foundations for future success.

If you are working with others, sweat equity can become a more complex issue. In a company, where one person stumps up the money and the other does all the preparatory work, for example, the partners need to work out how their different commitments count when it comes to dividing up shares.

Community choice

Community Development Finance Institutions (CDFIs) are another source of ethical finance. These are generally smaller lenders rooted in particular communities. Some are linked by their localities, like Blackpool Moneyline, or by racial or ethnic ties, such as the Ethnic Business Development Corporation.

CDFIs have both social and financial objectives, so they won't be surprised to find you do too. They may often be the last port of call for an enterprise which has been turned down elsewhere. Unlike other lenders, which may offer a range of different finance options, CDFIs typically only provide loans. But they don't just deal in small numbers. According to their umbrella association, these community banks have a combined total of £450 million to lend and invest. In 2005, they made loans of £181 million; a 23 per cent increase on the previous year.

The London Rebuilding Society is one of the largest CDFIs in the UK. Its loan finance options include the Assistance and Business Loans for Ethical Enterprise (ABLE) fund, targeted specifically at socially and environmentally responsible enterprises which find it difficult to raise finance through conventional banks. ABLE loans range from £5,000 to £50,000 and are open to businesses that meet one of the following criteria:

■ Have an ethical product or service (fair trade, green transport, renewable energy, fuel economy products, recycling, organics, regeneration, services targeted at under-represented groups)

■ Have an ethical, social or environmental purpose

London Rebuilding Society
www.londonrebuilding.com

An independent funding organisation, which lends re-payable loans to businesses that create jobs and opportunities supporting local communities.

▓ Are consciously disability led, women led, or Black and minority ethnic led

▓ Create employment opportunities for local people, people with disabilities, young people and other disadvantaged groups

▓ Are inner-city businesses committed to investing in their community

▓ Are concerned with property-based regeneration

▓ Are concerned with affordable housing

▓ Have a policy to invest a percentage of their profit in ethical, social or charitable purposes

▓ Have a strong stakeholder representation but are profit making

If you are planning to give a percentage of your profits to international development projects, a CDFI could be your best source of loan finance.

Measuring risk

Notwithstanding their strong affinity to ethical business, however, CDFIs are also very concerned about risk. After all, the more money they lose in unsuccessful ventures, the harder it is for them to carry out their community-based objectives.

"It is very difficult for us to tell in the early stages whether the business will cover all of its costs," admits Bruce Wood, loans manager at London Rebuilding Society. "So without a track record, it is hard (for a new business) to break through. What people need to do is spend enough time looking at whether the market exists for their idea. And even if such a business is feasible, it's essential that they look at it over time, understand how long it will take them to break even and also recoup any losses. If they can show all that, it will improve their chances."

Such is the lack of planning shown by many loan applicants, community lenders like London Rebuilding Society have had to resort to running special training programmes to get people "investment ready". Ironically, many community banks have plenty of money they want to lend, but they cannot find suitably secure ventures in which to invest.

So if you're serious about running a financially viable ethical business, you might consider taking them up on this training package. Not only will you benefit from financial workshops and one-to-one coaching, you could also be awarded financial support at the end of it.

Ethical funds

Depending on your legal form, there may be other sources of capital specifically geared to your business. Ethical lenders **Industrial Common Ownership Finance** and **Co-operative Action Loan Fund**, for example, provide a range of loan finance aimed primarily at co-operatives and employee-owned businesses.

One of the biggest advantages of the new Community Interest Company (CIC) form (see p.126) is that your business will be eligible for many loan and grant funds normally reserved for charities.

Here are some of the biggest ethical funds:

The **Local Investment Fund** operates regional community loan funds of between £15,000 and £100,000 throughout England. The scheme is only open to ethical enterprises that reinvest all of their profits back into the business/community, or have adopted the new CIC structure. Many of their clients are charities set up as companies limited by guarantee.

Futurebuilders is a vast, government-backed fund aimed at helping social enterprises deliver better public services. Futurebuilders has £125 million at its disposal for loans and grant funding, but there

Futurebuilders
www.futurebuilders-
england.org.uk

A government-backed £125 million investment fund, which provides a combination of loans, grants and support for organisations that deliver public services.

Finance ready?

Want to impress the bank manager? Here are London Rebuilding Society's top tips for loan applicants:

■ Your business plan must be accurate, believable and complete

■ Your financial projections include break-even and sales forecasts, and cash flow

■ All of these are based on sound assumptions and show best- and worst-case scenarios

■ You are clear about all the costs involved in running your venture

■ You know a lot about your customers and what motivates them to buy from you

■ You are aware of your competitors and have worked out a strategy to deal with them

■ You can show clearly how your social aims are central to your enterprise

■ You can show how you will manage and organise your board or management committee

■ You know which legal structure you have chosen and why

www.londonrebuilding.com

Adventure Capital Fund
www.adventurecapitalfund.
org.uk

Government funding
and support scheme,
which invests in local
communities by helping
organisations to be more
sustainable.

England's Regional
Development Agencies
www.englandsrdas.com

A government initiative,
consisting of nine
regional bodies which
have a commitment to
transforming England
through sustainable
economic development.

BIGinvest
www.biginvest.co.uk

A Big Issue magazine
funding initiative, which
helps finance social
enterprises.

are strict restrictions on who can apply. Its eligibility checklist insists applicants are "clearly constituted for public or community benefit" and not able "to dispose of assets for private gain – except as permitted for Community Interest Companies".

Happily, other potential funders are less stringent. The **Adventure Capital Fund** (ACF) is a joint venture between the government and Regional Development Agencies (public bodies charged with increasing economic prosperity). The fund provides mentoring and financial help to businesses with "a track record of delivering to [their] community". Its finance packages are extremely diverse. The ACF can loan money for start-up and product development, to help cash flow and stock financing, and for more major investments, such as purchasing a building. These "patient" loans (see opposite) are typically long-term, low interest and don't require a guarantee.

As well as loans, the ACF also offers a profit-share arrangement; if your business trains refugees to make and sell ethnic clothes, you might be offered investment based on a royalty agreement, where repayment is based on sales. If your business is judged to have a very strong social benefit, you might also be eligible for gift capital, which does not have to be repaid.

The Big Issue is one of the most famous ethical businesses in the UK. On the back of the street paper's success, it set up **BIGinvest** to help other socially responsible enterprises buy and develop property or raise working capital for good purposes. BIGinvest has access to £3.5 million pounds of loan funding. To qualify, you need to demonstrate strong management, a "projected ability to meet loan payments from cash flows" and meet the fund's key ethical criteria: to serve disadvantaged areas or people, or focus on environmental, ethical or community regeneration.

JARGON BUSTING... Patient capital

Some funders will give ethical businesses a better loan deal in exchange for guaranteed social or environmental outputs. This preferential finance is known as "patient capital".

Here, the word "patient" refers to the length of time that funders will normally wait until they are repaid.

CDFIs, for instance, can offer a variety of flexible packages on much more favourable terms than any high-street finance. Examples of patient capital schemes include:

■ low or zero interest loans
■ partial loan repayment through in-kind services
■ more time given to repay interest

Microfinance

If you need external finance and the banks won't help, you may be able to apply for a smaller chunk of money (usually between a few hundred and a couple of thousand pounds), which will still enable you to get your business off the ground.

Incredit is a Hertfordshire-based CDFI which offers one-to-one business support and training workshops to new entrepreneurs. Anyone who completes their Enterprise Training programme is also eligible to apply for a Micro Finance Business Start-Up Loan, up to a maximum of £1,000 repayable over 12 to 18 months.

Microfinance schemes are usually operated locally. Check with your nearest business centre, and visit the Community Development Finance Association (CDFA) website to find out more.

Community Development Finance Association
www.cdfa.org.uk

A trade association for independent financial institutions which provide capital and support to sustainable organisations in disadvantaged communities.

Overdrafts

Going into the red on your bank account might not seem like the wisest way to finance your business, but an agreed overdraft with your bank can be a useful method of accessing capital quickly. The pay-off for this flexibility is that overdrafts invariably work out to be quite expensive (more costly than a loan) and you can be asked to repay them at any time. For this reason, they should be seen as a kitty to help negotiate cash-flow problems, not your main source of finance. Overdrafts are typically secured on an enterprise's assets. If you don't have any, your bank manager might be unwilling to help out. Social banks are more likely to listen to ethical businesses, however. Unity Trust Bank, for example, has an overdraft facility designed especially for social enterprises and charities that are waiting to receive grant funding.

Credit cards

Banks never part with their money lightly, but credit card companies are practically falling over themselves for your business. Credit cards are quick and easy ways to raise finance. Handled well, they can also be very effective. If you can spot and juggle a few good low interest deals, you may need never step into a loan manager's office again. What's the catch? Interest rates on credit cards are usually much higher than those on bank loans. If you don't keep a close watch on your cash flow situation and fail to pay bills off on time, debts can rapidly spiral out of control.

You may also have ethical reasons for not wanting to go down this route. Credit card debt in the UK reached £54.7 billion in summer 2006, with

3.4 million cardholders regularly making only the minimum repayment – thereby maximising their interest charges. Among these cardholders are some of the most vulnerable people in society, trapped in debt because irresponsible banks have offered them large amounts of credit. If you feel strongly about this, you may want to avoid the plastic. Alternatively, you could decide to only use credit cards from ethical banks, such as Smile.

Hire purchase

You can get pretty much anything these days on a Hire Purchase (HP) deal. If you need to buy a vehicle, for example, to deliver your organic produce to the shops, rather than taking one big hit on your credit card, HP means you can start using expensive equipment straightaway while paying it off slowly. The usual method is monthly instalments, at the end of which you have the option of owning the goods outright. HP is a great way to free up much-needed cash, but the payback is the added expense. You pay interest on top of the agreed price. These rates can vary wildly and don't forget to check any extra charges before signing on the dotted line.

Factoring

One of the biggest headaches for any new business is managing the gap between providing goods or services and getting paid by customers. If you run an eco-tourism business, you may not receive any money from holidaymakers until several weeks after you have had to pay the holiday providers. If your finances are otherwise healthy, factoring is a relatively simple way to address this problem. Every time you write an invoice, you send it to the factoring company (either banks or specialist firms), who immediately advance up to 85 per cent of the bill. Once the customer pays, you get the rest, less an agreed percentage charge. The precise charge for this varies, but it is usually similar to an overdraft.

Shares

Depending on your legal form, you may be able to raise money by selling shares in your business. The big advantage is that this "equity" capital – unlike debt – does not have to be repaid. To some degree, this makes shares a less risky form of finance than loans. If your company is struggling, you would still be expected to keep up loan repayments. But shareholders will only expect any dividends if your business is turning a profit.

In the long run, however, selling shares could turn out to be a much greater sacrifice. Every time you sell a share, you give away a percentage of the business. Not only does this impact on who actually runs the enterprise, it could also affect who profits from your hard work. If your company booms, you may see much of the spoils go to a canny investor who snapped up early shares for a bargain.

Unless you are a listed company, remember this kind of share issue has nothing to do with the stock exchange. Unlisted companies limited by shares (or any of the other share-issuing forms, such as co-operatives and CICs) are only allowed to make a private share issue. You can create any number of shares at any value. Depending on the share price you set, this can raise considerable sums of money.

The government's **Enterprise Investment Scheme** is designed to encourage this kind of finance. Provided that shares are held for up to three years, investors can get 20 per cent tax relief. In other words, a £10,000 investment should actually only cost £8,000.

Realistically, however, many start-ups will be lucky to convince anyone but their friends and family that they are a worthy investment. As the founder, you may end up owning 100 per cent of the shares. Which may not be a bad thing.

Keeping control

The big disadvantage of selling shares is control. Every share you release to a third party is a portion of your business. Sell more than 50 per cent and you have lost overall ownership of the company. As an ethical business, this could seriously compromise your core values. If majority shareholders decide the company should reduce its commitment to dealing with its carbon footprint, you may have no power to stop them.

That said, there are ways to integrate your ethical principles into any share issue. Sometimes called Ethical Public Offerings (EPOs), these can be used to safeguard your core values, and give customers or other stakeholders, such as suppliers, a real sense of ownership of the company.

In recent years, fair trade companies Cafédirect and Traidcraft, and the Ethical Property Company, have done just that. When Cafédirect raised share finance, it decided to involve its customers and producers directly in the running of the business. The four founding organisations reduced their shareholding to 39 per cent, with five per cent of shares being passed to producer groups who also elect two of Cafédirect's directors. Other investors and consumers can elect one director to the board, but no individual can own more than 15 per cent of the company. This innovative restructuring has brought everyone from UK shoppers to developing world growers together without compromising the business's ethical direction.

"It's a stakeholder approach," Cafédirect CEO Penny Newman told journalists after the share issue. "We want to take consumers and producers with us. They're going to be shaping our way forward."

Angels and venture capital

If you've ever watched an episode of Dragons' Den, you'll know what a business angel looks like. Angels are wealthy individuals who put up capital in return for a percentage of your business. That may sound frightening, but giving away a portion of the company could actually be a less risky strategy than a debt, which could be called in at any time. No two angels are the same. Some prefer to be "sleeping partners": they won't get involved in the business at all. Others will be more hands-on. Given their wealth of experience and contacts, this is often no bad thing. If you attract a group of angels working as a syndicate, you may suddenly have a string of expert advisors at your disposal.

Ethical businesses are often attractive propositions for angels. After careers spent chasing little else but profits, many are looking for something more meaningful to support. That doesn't mean they are in it for charity, however. Angels and venture capitalists will only support companies they consider to be high growth, well managed and that offer them a well-

Fair share?

How much money you can raise from a share issue will depend on your legal structure. Here are the key factors to consider:

Company Limited by Shares

Easily the most flexible form. A private share issue, whether to a few friends or a dozen or so investors, can raise serious money. You can divide these up into ordinary and preference shares. Ordinary shares come with voting rights, however. If you sell 51 per cent or more of the shares, you could lose control of the business.

Company Limited by Guarantee

Very simple. CLGs cannot issue shares.

Community Interest Company

With a capped maximum return, CICs are not the most attractive proposition for investors. Nevertheless, smaller ethical investors, who have a strong belief in your goals, may be willing to stump up the cash.

Industrial and Provident Societies

If you register a co-operative as an IPS, or start up a BenCom (see p.129) you can issue shares of up to £20,000 per investor.

BenComs can raise very large share issues at relatively low cost, but their profits are tightly regulated so it's not a great deal for the investor. IPS-structured co-operatives have much fewer restrictions on dividends, but find it much more expensive to raise very large share issues. In both cases, investors get one vote, regardless of how much they have invested.

defined exit strategy. Most investors will be looking to move on in three to eight years.

The right angel

If you want to raise larger sums (e.g. £250,000 or more), business advisors P3 Capital and social bank Triodos have access to wealthy private investors who

P3 Capital
www.p3capital.com

A corporate advisory firm which works with entrepreneurs and companies with social and environmental aims.

are looking to invest in ethical companies. They can also help you develop your strategy and assist you in getting investment ready by working with you in preparing your business plan. Typically the investors they introduce will still be looking to make good financial returns out of their investments, but are likely to be more sympathetic to your social and environmental goals than regular business angels. Alternatively, there are a number of mainstream business angel networks around the country to whom you can apply. If selected, you will be able to present your business to their angel investors. Networks operate in different ways, but they will normally charge a percentage of the funds you raise and an upfront fee for presenting.

Venture capitalists

As a rule, business angels are better suited to start-ups and small businesses than professional venture capital (VC) companies. Most angels will be looking to invest between £10,000 and £750,000. VC groups usually work in six-figure sums only.

There are, however, some schemes aimed specifically at smaller businesses:

The **Early Growth Fund**, for example, is an innovative "matching" scheme aimed at innovative growth businesses. If you can secure private investment (either through an angel, venture capitalist or other investor), the ECG can match that investment, up to a maximum of £100,000.

Regional Venture Capital Funds recognise that smaller businesses struggle to attract VC. An England-wide programme, it provides up to £500,000 of professionally managed investment to high potential, small and medium-sized companies.

Thanks to the boom in ethical investment, there is also a growing number of VC funds aimed specifically at ethical businesses. Besides **Bridges Community Ventures** (see below), London-based equity company **Foursome** offers early-stage investment opportunities for "innovative growth businesses seeking to create a positive social and environmental impact – as well as achieve significant financial returns."

If you get it right on the day, the rewards can be huge. After 20 bank branches had refused them funding, Jon Wright, Adam Balon and Richard Reed of Innocent Drinks began emailing friends to ask if they knew anyone rich. That's how they met wealthy American businessman, Maurice Pinto. They pitched to his venture capital fund, but were turned down. After a further two-hour grilling, however, Pinto was impressed and decided to lend them £230,000 of his own money.

Ethical dragons?

Bridges Community Ventures is an innovative venture capital company which invests in ambitious businesses located in the most economically disadvantaged parts of England.

In 2002, Bridges decided to invest £125,000 in utilities price comparison start-up SimplySwitch. As a result of the investment, the company located itself in a deprived south London ward, and has since created more than 80 jobs for local people. As part of its social contribution programme, the company has also raised more than £500,000 for charity.

After its first offer was accepted, Bridges later increased its investment to £345,000 and worked closely with the management team to grow the business. Its strategy worked. In 2006, SimplySwitch was bought out for £22 million.

www.bridgesventures.com

The right equity

According to leading US funding directory Business Finance, when professional venture capital firms ask about your previous ventures, "they're only interested in the bottom line". They don't care if the companies help the community, create jobs or protect the environment.

By contrast, angel investors often fund companies "for motives that may not be purely financial". Some want to put something back into the industries that made them successful. Others want to help new businesses over the hurdles that they struggled with in the early days, or may have a particular cause close to their hearts.

Grants

Free money probably sounds like heaven. If you are running your business along ethical principles, there is every chance that you could be eligible for some kind of grant finance. Most grants are aimed at charities, but a small number of grants are also available for companies. As an ethical entrepreneur, you can sometimes skate between these two lines and enjoy the best of both worlds.

If you start a marketing consultancy which offers pro bono help to first-time entrepreneurs from disadvantaged communities, you may be eligible for a variety of grants: from small start-up funds available to all new businesses, through to specific grant schemes aimed solely at businesses and organisations that make a direct contribution to a specific social problem.

Free money?

While this might seem to be a bonus, in reality, grants are rarely the quick buck they first appear. They can be extremely useful as an extra cash injection – especially when no one else looks like stumping up the money – but they may also have other dangers: such as steering your business away from its original purpose and creating a financial dependency.

Sometimes the biggest hurdle can seem to be the application itself. Grant forms are notoriously long-winded, tedious and occasionally downright incomprehensible. The money on offer can seem like a fair reward just for filling one out.

Nevertheless, providing that you are managing your time carefully – and not becoming a slave to application forms – it's worth investigating what schemes are open to you.

Grant awards exist for a huge variety of enterprises: eligibility criteria can depend on your age, where you're setting up, what kind of business you're running, and a host of other conditions. Thankfully, there are a number of excellent search engines, such as **www.j4b.co.uk**, into which you can enter all your business details and find out what you can apply for. Your local Business Link will also be able to point you in the right direction.

The **New Entrepreneur Scholarship Programme** is an example of a grant locked into particular locations. People living in particularly disadvantaged areas can apply for support and funding of up to £1,500 to support their growth. Applications from ethically minded businesses are especially welcome.

New Entrepreneur Scholarship Programme
www.nesprogramme.org

Government initiative which offers funding and support to people living in disadvantaged areas to start in business.

If your idea is still at a very early stage – or you have opted against incorporation – **UnLtd** is a charity that supports individuals, not companies. It has two tiers of grant-giving aimed at "people with vision, drive, commitment and passion who want to change the world for the better". Level 1 awards (between £500 and £5,000) are given to help make new ideas become real projects; Level 2 awards pay for new entrepreneurs' living expenses to help them devote more time to their projects.

UnLtd has a strong track record of supporting innovative ethical ideas. An UnLtd Level 1 grant award was how Grant Lang managed to turn his idea for solar- and wind-powered, art-covered coffee carts into reality. Today his company, Mozzo, sells its own blend of fair trade, organic coffee via a growing number of environmentally friendly carts and through local retailers in Southampton.

Business Gateway

www.bgateway.com

Scottish Executive partnership, which offers information, funding and support to start-up businesses in Scotland.

For young start-up entrepreneurs in Scotland, **Business Gateway** currently offers a £1,000 grant to help you get your business off the ground. Besides the cash, you will also receive free business advice on everything from e-commerce to international trading.

Historically, the **European Social Fund** (ESF) has been one of the largest grant providers to UK businesses. But in recent years, as new member states join the EU, the British pot has been getting smaller. In January 2007, ESF changed its rules and warns "there will be less funding now for richer member states such as the UK".

Under the new EU rules, there are now two kinds of grants available:

"Convergence Objective" is only available for businesses in Cornwall and the Isles of Scilly, and West Wales and the Valleys. (Companies in the Highlands and Islands of Scotland may also qualify for "phasing out" Convergence funding.)

The even less catchy "Regional Competitiveness and Employment Objective" is earmarked for projects which increase competitiveness, employment and skills in regions that are not eligible for the Convergence Objective.

While the pots of funding are still huge (£1.7 billion and £4.2 billion respectively), the overall trend is clear. With so many economically less wealthy member states than the UK, EU resources are increasingly being diverted elsewhere. Those who had come to expect healthy annual hand-outs from the EU are suddenly facing a funding shortfall.

The **Department of Trade and Industry** (DTI) is a handy source of information for many grants. If your business is involved in researching and developing technologically innovative products or processes, for example, you may be eligible for any manner of DTI grant funding: from micro-project support up to £20,000, through to complete development project funding up to £200,000.

These and other grants are available via **Regional Development Agencies**, a network of organisations which support regional economic development and regeneration around the UK.

Grants more geared to charities include **The Big Lottery Fund**, which supports organisations that are committed to making their communities stronger. Applications are often open to "businesses that [are] chiefly run for social objectives". One successful organisation is Furniture Now! which runs a community recycling service and trains people with mental health needs to refurbish second-hand furniture, which it sells at low cost to people in East Sussex. Furniture Now! received £184,907 from The Big Lottery Fund in 2003. Today, it provides more than 3,500 households and

The Big Lottery Fund
www.biglotteryfund.org.uk

Hands out about £630 million of lottery money annually to various sustainable business projects.

Esmée Fairbairn Foundation

www.esmeefairbairn.org.uk

One of the largest independent grant making organisations in the UK, which funds projects that aim to improve the quality of life for people and communities.

Community Action Network

www.can-online.org.uk

Support and networking organisation set up by three social entrepreneurs to help other ethical businesses transform deprived communities.

voluntary groups with low-cost furniture and recycles more than 900 tonnes of household waste.

The **Esmée Fairbairn Foundation** made grants of approximately £29 million across the UK in 2006. One of its initiatives, the Social Change: Enterprise and Independence programme, is aimed specifically at ethical business. There is a long list of enterprises they won't consider supporting, but it's worth checking their website to see if you qualify.

Community Action Network (CAN), an incubator of different support services for socially-motivated entrepreneurs, has set up a new grant award for more established social enterprises. Applicants for its Breakthrough scheme have to demonstrate a minimum of three years' trading history and a profitable, scalable business model. In return, they can receive grant funding with a "venture capital" style support package. Successful applicants not only get the money, but they can also tap into expert business advice from CAN and their funding partner, private equity firm Permira.

If you are finding it hard to raise money elsewhere, a grant award could be just the break you need. But there are dangers too. Developing a grant habit could seriously damage your long-term ambitions.

The grant trap

How can free money be harmful? Uday Thakkar, director of business consultancy Red Ochre, runs a workshop on how to wean ethical enterprises off grant finance. "Once you get in, it becomes a trap," he explains. "It can create a drift from your mission, make you short-termist and undervalue human capital."

Most grants have strings attached, effectively telling you how the money is to be spent. This may not tie in with your own opinion on the matter. Successful grant awards, for example, are often earmarked for a particular project.

If you are starting a door-to-door service to help householders reduce their carbon footprint, you may first need to train up staff or create a website to help generate business. But if you have won a grant award, you may find that the money can only be spent on carbon reduction projects. If you can't afford to meet the training and website costs separately, you may not be able to prepare the business properly. You might have a pot of money, but you can't use it where it most needs to be spent. This is clearly not how anyone would normally do business.

In addition, if the funding is limited to 12 months, you have only a short time to secure more capital to ensure the project can continue. Unless you do this quickly, your employees will start wondering how safe their jobs are and begin looking elsewhere.

"The way the cycle works, you might already be a few months into the project before you've got the [grant] money and can recruit people," explains Uday. "Six months later, those same people are already looking to get out. If they go, whatever learning they've gained from the project leaves too."

Mission drift is where you gradually lose sight of your original purpose. Grants can affect this because you may be awarded money for only one part of your business. As the enterprise becomes more dependent on this "free" finance, the whole organisation becomes unnaturally skewed towards the grant-generating element of the enterprise; before long, it can no longer survive independently.

If your business designs and sells affordable products which can improve the lives of deaf people around the world, you may receive a large amount of funding to help finance your research and development (R&D) work. If this is the only area of the business which attracts grants, however, you may end up chasing this free money – by reducing, or even scrapping, everything other than your R&D operations. This may have negative implications on your finances and your ethics: not only could you become dependent on what is ultimately an unreliable source of finance (could your R&D business survive if the grants suddenly dried up, for example?), but without any sales or distribution arm, considerably fewer of your products may ever get to the people who really need them.

Short-term grants can be equally diverting for the people running the business. If you are frantically trying to secure more grants every year, or reporting back on how you've spent previous awards, it affects the time you can spend running the business. Another characteristic of grant awards is that they are often geared towards the most glamorous projects. There is a lot more cachet, for example, involved in funding a new technology than supporting a retailer who sells it on to the masses.

There may be times when your only source of funding is through grants. Depending on your legal structure and your ability to pull in finances elsewhere, they can be a crucial source of capital. Ideally, however, they should be an added extra – just one element of your finance mix. The acid test is if the grant money were suddenly pulled away, could your business survive? If it couldn't, you are no longer in control of your own destiny; if you don't keep winning those grant awards, your business will fail. If grants are your only finance option for the first couple of months or even years, remember that generating your own revenue should always be the ultimate goal. Only financial self-sufficiency can give you the control, confidence and freedom to set your ethical business on a steady course to success.

Zaytoun: Banking on oil

When ethical olive oil company Zaytoun began selling to UK customers in 2005, founders Cathi Davis and Heather Gardner immediately faced a cash-flow problem.

Originally a voluntary organisation, Zaytoun aims to raise living standards for Palestinian olive growers by building up a fair and sustainable export industry. Currently, more than half the olive oil produced in Palestine is thrown away due to a lack of access to international markets.

Zaytoun was set up to make a difference. But one of the guiding principles of fair trade is early payment to producers. Despite having £15,000 of orders from people who wanted the oil, the business could therefore not begin trading until it had raised sufficient capital.

In spring 2005, Cathi and Heather approached Triodos bank for funding. After presenting their business plan, they were awarded a £25,000 loan. "Triodos supported not only our finances but our aims and values," says Cathi. "The loan allowed us to pay the Palestinian farmers for enough oil to meet fast-growing demand in the UK."

Before contacting Triodos, the founders had spent a long time researching the olive oil market. They had also trained themselves in basic accounting, and attended networking sessions. These helped them to get to know a number of fair trade experts, who effectively became their business mentors.

One of the mentors was former chairman of Cafédirect, Martin Meteyard. When Triodos asked for financial guarantors for the loan, he was one of the people to underwrite £5,000.

Looking back, Heather says that having other signatures made a big difference. "Taking out £25,000 felt like a huge risk for us at the time. But having financial guarantors definitely made us feel a lot better."

Thanks to the loan, coupled with a £6,000 grant by international development charity War on Want, Zaytoun has been able to commit to increasingly large orders. In 2005, it sold three times more Palestinian olive oil than in the previous year. It is currently on the way to both organic and full Fairtrade certification.

www.zaytoun.org

10 Spreading the Word

IN THIS CHAPTER...

▓ **How to create an ethical PR strategy**

▓ **How to approach the media**

▓ **Where to promote your ethics**

If your business is trying to be as sustainable and fair as possible, don't be shy. Telling the world about your company is a great way to communicate your core beliefs, increase public understanding of the big issues and bring new customers to your business.

There has never been a better time to show off your credentials. Ethical consumerism has been steadily growing for the last six years and shows no sign of slowing down. In 2005, global sales in fair trade products soared by a massive 37 per cent to £758 million. In 2004, consumers spent £3.4 billion on trying to tackle climate change, and invested more than £10 billion in ethical investments.

The message is clear: if you have a great ethical business idea, you are appealing to a rapidly expanding market. This trend has not gone unnoticed, which explains the increase in companies pretending to be ethical. If you are the genuine article, you need to make sure that you are shouting the loudest.

Mirror, mirror

Before calling the papers, start with your own image. If you're selling a product, your packaging is a canvas to present your public face. Not only is it free advertising space for your logo and slogan, you can also make any materials used as environmentally friendly as possible.

Organic food box delivery company Abel & Cole underlines its commitment to locally produced food by having the slogan "Zero air miles – we never freight" emblazoned on its food boxes. Also prominent is the logo of the Queen's Award for Enterprise, where it was recognised for its achievements in sustainable development in 2005. The packaging itself is also part of the business's ethical make-up: Abel & Cole encourages customers to leave out their used cardboard boxes for the company to collect and re-use.

Your website is another opportunity to showcase your brand. The homepage for ethical bottled water company Belu, for example, features its product next to the line: "The UK's first compostable bottle! Made from corn!" The surrounding text reads "All our profits go to clean water projects – every bottle you drink gives someone clean water for a month!" and: "Belu is the first water company that doesn't contribute to climate change".

On just one neatly designed page, the company's key ethical messages are clearly presented. Click an arrow in the bottom corner and the website jumps to a series of flash-animated pages, explaining global water issues and all of Belu's eco-friendly initiatives.

Once your own house is in order, you can move onto contacting the wider world. If you get it right, the results can be astonishing. Organic chocolate manufacturer Green & Black's was awarded Marketer of the Year for 2005 by the Marketing Society and Marketing magazine after it achieved 70 per cent growth in 2004. In that same year, the chocolate industry as a whole grew by only two per cent.

One of the keys to Green & Black's achievement was strong marketing. The company admits that promoting its ethical attributes helped it to make the jump from niche health food stores into major supermarkets.

There are dozens of ways to build an effective PR strategy: leafleting, printing catalogues and taking out small advertisements are just some of the most common approaches. There may be ethical factors to consider, though. When it comes to printing, for example, you might want to insist on recycled paper or paper from well-managed forests (see p.200). You could also decide to use ethical printers, such as Marc the Printers in Manchester or the Calverts co-operative in London, which have worked hard to minimise their environmental impact. If you still feel uncomfortable about the idea of printing thousands of leaflets, you could try to use email as much as possible. To target a specific market, you could buy mailing lists from specialist brokerage services. If you need to build a pool of qualified lawyers who will donate time and expertise to help disadvantaged communities, for example, you might only want to target the legal profession.

Setting up your website to accept internet sales is another way to enhance your appeal and accessibility. It could even drastically alter the way you run as a company.

Today, 94 per cent of ethical fashion brand Howies' business comes from its website and catalogue sales. But only a few years ago, that figure was 50 per cent, and the company was spending a lot of time, effort and money trying to sell its clothes through other shops. Understanding where its marketing strategy was most effective has been crucial to making the business run more efficiently.

If you decide to use an outside company to help you devise your PR strategy, you may also want their values to fit your own. Ethical PR companies, such as St Lukes, Koan and Futerra, are committed to strong social objectives, such as supporting community development projects and giving free expertise to voluntary groups. An ethical PR company may also be selective about its client base. If you start a cruelty-free cosmetics business, you may decide you won't use a PR company which also accepts work from companies that use animal testing.

PR

Creating a buzz about your ethical enterprise is one of the most exciting ways to boost a new business. Get it right and you can increase custom, test your business model and get valuable feedback about the services and products on offer. Over the following pages, ethical PR company Koan gives its advice on how to spread the word, without getting in a spin.

Anyone starting a new business has a thousand things to think about. And an ethical business leader probably has more than most. A business shaped by values (rather than just value) may have even more rigorous operating decisions to make, not least when it comes to generating PR with a purpose. In promoting a company with a conscience, it's not necessarily true that "any publicity is good publicity".

If you need to print a catalogue for your fair trade clothes company, simply choosing the cheapest option could risk your entire reputation. If a journalist discovers that your printer's cheap prices come off the back of sweatshop labour and poor environmental standards, you could find yourself branded a hypocrite in the papers. If you're going to promote your business as ethical, you need to make sure it really is.

Then there's the start-up struggle to stay viable. Sustainable business development involves constant nurturing. While living those ethics continues far beyond the initial launch phase, that first crucial growth spurt may draw on all your energy reserves. It's hardly surprising that so many young enterprises neglect to feed media interest, when just keeping afloat is a struggle.

Think positive

And yet... the effort really is worthwhile. PR is more than a feel-good, self-promotional, get your face in the paper activity, although it can certainly achieve that too. In deft hands, it's a powerful business tool that can deliver both rapid rewards and long-term profits. Even before your ethical enterprise launches, it's important to make contact with people who influence public opinion. And the faster you can mobilise your media relations team (even if it's only you), the sooner you'll get the town, city or the web talking.

If you're still mistrustful of the media and those

who seek to manipulate it, remember that despite its often tawdry reputation, PR can be enterprising and ethical. In its truest sense, public relations is a great opportunity to create a positive impact. It can drive footfall through the door and raise socially important issues. It can position your company as the business to trust and help you to engage more closely with the community. Given the media's unprecedented interest in all things ethical, there has also never been a better time to explain your goals. Many socially minded enterprises have developed highly innovative ways to address particular problems, and these can often make for a great story. When it comes to getting publicity, your ethical business could therefore have a clear PR advantage over a run-of-the-mill company which is only interested in making profit for its directors and shareholders.

There need be no contradiction between doing good things through your business and generating great stories in the media. Like any ethical choice in life, it's not just what you do, it's the way that you do it that counts.

Budgeting resources

Whether you engage a PR consultancy or dedicate your own time to a campaign, PR delivers more bang for your budget than advertising could hope to achieve. The Chartered Institute of Public Relations estimates that editorial coverage is worth almost four times the value of advertising space. Why? Because editorial is seen as more authentic. Viewers trust and absorb editorial messages on a deeper level than they respond to the direct selling messages in adverts.

Given the amount of advertising space you could afford to buy as a young business, you are likely to gain more column inches – and more impact per inch – by securing editorial coverage. The beauty of PR is that you can achieve a great deal with relatively few resources. Work smart to identify your most important media targets, then direct tailored approaches to the right people and you could gain valuable coverage that proves strategically important to your business.

If you start an organic food box scheme which helps to train people with learning disabilities and provides them with jobs, you might want to contact not just the national press, but also specialist publications, such as food magazines, agricultural titles, business magazines, and publications specifically for disabled people and those working in the disability sector. There are also a number of specialist ethical magazines (see opposite), which may be interested in your story.

Setting objectives

It may sound obvious, but being very focused on your PR objectives will help to deliver the quality of coverage you need to create genuine business impact. Unless you're happy to conduct a PR campaign purely to flatter egos and prompt mutual back-slapping (which can be fun but not very effective) you need to understand and agree your PR aims and objectives. By focusing on just two or three major priorities, these main motivators can help to shape your campaign. Objectives may include:

Green Pages

The growing media appetite for all things ethical means that you now have an ever increasing number of outlets through which to showcase your business.

Almost every national newspaper now has an ethical living column, environment section or society pages. Contacting the editors of these sections directly can frequently be more productive than firing off press releases to the main news desk. Magazines too – from glossy women's titles to business-to-business monthlies – have never been more switched on to green issues. So if you run an ethical fashion brand, don't be afraid to tell everyone from Vogue to your local newspaper all about it.

If social and environmental aims run through the heart of your business, you may have several different angles to your story. If you run a "carbon neutral" IT company, and donate 10 per cent of profits to overseas development projects, your story could justifiably fit into the technology, business, society or environmental section. This flexibility will give you more options when it comes to getting noticed.

The surge in ethical consumerism has also led to a growing number of online and print magazines specialising in ethical shopping. Titles such as New Consumer and Ethical Consumer are always on the look out for innovative new ethical companies to bring to their readerships. If you can convince them to feature your product or service, your business could soon be the talk of the town.

■ Expressing your brand personality, values and motivations

■ Attracting the attention of a specific target audience

■ Driving footfall into the store

■ Driving click-through to the website

■ Engaging with specific groups within the community

■ Positioning your ethical business as a unique enterprise

■ Increasing the volume and value of sales

■ Raising awareness of a social issue which has inspired your business

■ Affecting consumer behaviour and prompting direct action

■ Influencing decision-makers within private and public sector organisations

Developing messages

Before you start a campaign, your key points should be defined and refined (and refined and refined), so that every business communication – from a simple press release to a full media launch – is true to your core messages.

Some ruthless PR practitioners get entangled in debates about the politics of spin, complaints about our celebrity-fuelled culture or accusations of greenwash. But this is the dirty side of PR. You can refine your core messages with a much more genuine purpose: to set out your stall, to clarify your ethical values, to communicate clearly and positively with your target audiences.

When securing media coverage or airtime, it is vital to keep these core messages in focus to ensure that – amidst all the excitement of a radio or newspaper interview – you don't forget to mention the most important point of all which is often simply your business name, mission and contact details. And when you send out a press release, that is your chance to really drive home the message, so make sure it is factually accurate and content rich.

Core messages will be entirely dependent on the nature of the business, but they could include your product or service offer, your ethical selling point and the benefits to your customer. The messages needn't be complicated. But they should be consistent, concise and memorable. Repetition is great. Rambling is not.

> " Just because you don't have any money to spend on marketing, doesn't mean you don't have to get it right. In fact, if you don't have any money, you have to get it extra right! "
>
> **Richard Reed,**
> **Innocent Drinks**

Relating to the media

Journalists are bombarded by press releases and phone calls from professional media relations executives with strenuous targets to hit. Blanket-bombing press releases via email is ubiquitous. More often than not, journalists click the delete button without a thought. You have seconds to impress.

For many PR professionals, securing coverage is a numbers game: the more calls you make, the greater your chances of a getting a "hit". The only problem is that making calls to 50 journalists in a day can tend to make you sound more like a telesales rep than a media mogul in the making.

Amidst this barrage of phone calls, your own approach needs to be fresh, intelligent and engaging. But then that's much easier when it is your own business: you have a real vision and you are excited about what you're doing. So enjoy your creative advantage. Remember that journalists love a good story, and to be ahead of a trend. That's why it's so important, not just to plug your product, but to make your story interesting and relevant to them. And most importantly to their readers.

What's so interesting about your story? As an ethical business, the way you run your business could be more interesting than your actual product or service. If you employ people with mental health issues to pack gift boxes, their stories will be much more interesting than the ribbon and cardboard – even if it is recycled.

Whatever your story, you need to pitch it appropriately. Local papers only want local interest stories and they are very specific about which areas and even neighbourhoods they cover. Higher circulation regional papers favour more significant business stories, human interest headlines and inspiration for lifestyle features. The nationals will want something really meaty to sink their teeth into. Proceed with caution.

Writing a press release

In an ideal world, a well-timed phone call may prompt a photographer to set out right away. But you will probably need to present your story several times over to get the coverage you desire. That's when a press release comes in useful. A press release is basically a written outline of your story, designed to whet the journalists' appetite for more.

You may have scoped out a beautifully detailed business plan or composed eloquent requests for funding. But when you're writing a press release, keep it brief rather than trying to pad out your story. Don't skimp on content, facts or figures, but do try to present them in the simplest way by following a clear structure.

Headline

If you want to make the headlines, the best way to start is by creating a few of your own. A headline is like your knock-em-dead outfit. It can win over your audience within seconds. Remember that most journalists are far too busy to read beyond your headline unless it's an instant hit. So headlines need to be short, clever and attention-grabbing.

If your organic breakfast delivery company, Rise'n'Shine, gives away any unsold food to homeless people every morning, you might come up with: "Organic Breakfasts Hit The Street".

Here are two tips to help you create your perfect headline:

1. Try writing your headline first. If a great one-liner occurs to you, you can use it to shape your whole press release.

2. If nothing comes, try writing your headline last. Sometimes only by writing your story will you discover the most important point for your headline. One way or another, you can overcome your writer's block.

The more news-focused your story, the more important it is that key facts (places, dates, names, etc.) are in the headline. But remember to consider your target media. The Daily Mirror's plea to "SAVE OUR SICK NHS" is a national tabloid's take on a campaign to boost the National Health Service. Your local paper will interpret the same story as, "Keep our maternity ward open". Know your audience and talk directly to them.

If you run a plumbing company in Clapton, east London, and give free support to charity and voluntary groups, you could keep the media informed about your latest projects. If you are doing pro bono work for a struggling children's charity, you might pitch: "London plumbers help charity stay afloat" to the national press and "Local plumbers pitch in to save St. Mathilda's" to local newspapers.

Opening

The first paragraph in any feature or press release should be no more than two or three lines long. Ideally it should summarise the main points of the whole piece, so that people can get the gist at a glance. Make these first lines as interesting as possible or you will lose your reader in the first few seconds.

Body

The main body of the press release or feature should continue to expand on the first couple of sentences, either explaining the story in a chronological way if you are recounting a particular event, or expanding on your main themes, e.g. the main selling points of your service or product. In the case of ethical breakfast company Rise'n'Shine, this might include more information about the wholesome quality of the food, the kind of nutritional problems homeless people often face and a snappy quote from a corporate customer to say how they have been won over not just by the delicious organic breakfasts, but also the strong social benefit.

Conclusion

Obviously there are certain things you need to include in any press release, such as contact details, facts and figures. But before you do this, you need to round off the press release as neatly as possible, by referring back to your headline, or summarising the main points. Don't just trail off as if you have lost interest.

Call to action

Finally, make sure you are clear what you want the reader to do as a result of reading. Do you want them to visit a website, start a fundraising drive, call for more information, support a charity? Whatever your goal is, be clear about this.

> ❝ We're not trying to preach to people. Making people feel shit about themselves is counter-productive. We don't agree with those sticker campaigns against SUV cars. If you stick a notice on people's windscreen telling them they're responsible for killing the planet, you will only piss them off. Probably the next car they'll buy will be another SUV. ❞
>
> **Tom Pakenham, Green Tomato Cars**

Perfect partnerships

When you're developing a new business concept, you may jealously guard your ideas through a natural fear of intellectual theft or copycat tactics. But when it comes to publicising your business, sharing your business vision with like-minded enterprises may actually work to mutual advantage.

A new fashion boutique selling fair trade, sweatshop-free and organic clothing, for example, recently teamed up with a well established co-operative grocery store and a new organic meat and dairy delicatessen to announce the creation of a new 'Fair Trade Triangle' in their local neighbourhood.

Collectively, the businesses gained far more coverage than they could hope to achieve alone, the journalist got a strong lifestyle feature angle and the readers enjoyed hearing about how they lived in a trendy yet socially conscious neighbourhood with great shops. Everyone was a winner.

Teaming up with other young businesses that share similarly ethical values can really help to make the media sit up and start paying attention. In isolation, they might see you as a lonely tub-thumping tree-hugger; together you're forward thinking trend setters. See how much nicer that feels?

Community initiatives

In the truest sense of the word, public relations is about how you interact with the outside world, not just how to manipulate the media. Getting involved in community initiatives is a very genuine way for your business to interact with your local population and actively demonstrate your brand values to potential consumers; it's also a great way to make your business more ethical.

Community projects can help to create a buzz and spread consumer awareness through word-of-mouth recommendations – a brilliant way to market your business, and entirely free too. Taking your business outside of its normal environment and into a realm of new, yet shared experiences can do much more for your business than an advert in the local paper.

As well as raising awareness and enhancing external perceptions of your ethical business, community initiatives can offer internal business benefits too, offering learning opportunities through the experience of engaging with particular groups of people and providing a forum for professional and personal development.

The beauty of getting involved in your community

is that you can choose to support an initiative that really floats your boat: ethically, creatively and strategically. You may want to take part in a food or arts festival, support a local fundraising drive, engage with a community group or help with tree planting or mentoring at a school – whatever is the best match with your enterprise and values. Both you and your community benefit, and your local paper might write a great story about it.

Stunts and events

While you may draw the line at traffic-stopping antics to publicise your new venture, devising a stunt could be the fastest way for a fledgling business to attract media attention.

Think in terms of great pictures: exciting action shots, not school-photo style line-ups. Sophistication is rarely the order of the day. For some reason, comedic costumes (man-size cat disguises, giant wigs and even full-body parsnip outfits) attract the flashlight. Likewise, outlandishly decorated cars, improbable inflatables and giant novelty cakes tend to turn heads. If you run an organic cheese company, you could build a massive cheeseboard (from reclaimed wood, of course) and fill it with your produce. A London-based marine conservation organisation might get people dressed as whales and dolphins to hand out leaflets along the Thames embankment.

Hopefully you can find more stylish ways to get your story covered, but that's down to you and your creative inspiration. Use your imagination without entirely forgetting your discretion and you may come up with a wild and wonderful idea that boosts your

CHECKLIST ✓
Spreading the word

☐ Maximise free media space, e.g. product, packaging, website

☐ Consider any ethical objections

☐ Set your PR objectives

☐ Create your core messages

☐ Prepare your press release

☐ Contact the media

☐ Create new partnerships

☐ Engage with your community

profits, without alienating your stakeholders.

If you're cringing at the thought of compromising your dignity for some easy publicity, there are other options. A well-planned event can provide the ideal forum to introduce your business to journalists and even broadcasters. Note the "well-planned" proviso: a disorganised and rushed event may do more harm than good.

An event gives you the perfect reason to make contact and build relationships with journalists, and it lends urgency to your story, helping to prioritise it as newsworthy. Whether it's an open day, a themed evening, a champagne reception or a hands-on workshop, a special event can provide a great platform to introduce your ethical business, especially if you work with like-minded partners to pull off a really exciting theme.

Media timescales

However you decide to approach PR for your business, it is vital to bear in mind the different timescales to which media channels work. It's pointless (even reckless) to disturb a journalist under deadline pressure. So you need to know when is a good time to call and when to keep a low profile. Journalists don't always work a standard five-day week – days off may depend on when the paper goes to print.

Too many fantastic coverage opportunities have been lost because the newspapers weren't alerted in time. To get coverage in a weekly local paper, make sure you contact them at least two weeks in advance. For daily regional papers, four days in advance is usually a safe bet. The monthly glossies are on a totally different timescale: regional magazines work two months in advance, while the nationals are working as much as three to four months ahead. As for national newspapers, feature material should be provided one to two weeks ahead, while the news desks work much faster to cover stories the next day.

Marketing on a shoestring

★ *When Innocent Drinks launched in 1999, they had no marketing budget at all. Today, they are a brand leader and have a turnover of £70 million. Director Richard Reed gives his top marketing tips for an ethical business on a tight budget.*

Use your core product
In the beginning, we didn't have a marketing budget. We said 95 per cent of our marketing strategy is what's in the bottle – something that's meaningfully better than the competition.

Grab every opportunity
Right from the start, our primary communication was constantly writing stuff on the back of our labels because that cost us nothing. We couldn't buy an advertising campaign, but we could write a great advert and put it on the label. That's the only bit of media space we owned.

Consistency and honesty count
To stand a chance of us getting noticed and remembered, we knew we had to be incredibly consistent. We've just been ourselves from day one and that's helped build consistency. We've not tried to appeal to different target audiences.

Put in the hours
Right from the start, we wanted to make sure the content on our website was as good as possible and consistently up-to-date. That took up our time, not money.

Be memorable
You need to think of interesting ways to communicate, which are also representative of your business. We needed to get our van branded so we did it in a memorable way (Innocent's vans are decorated to look like cows).

www.innocentdrinks.co.uk

11 Proving It

IN THIS CHAPTER...

- Why ethical accounting matters
- Where to find your stakeholders
- How to win ethical kitemarks

IT IS ONE thing to plan and start up your dream business. But what if someone challenged you on your ethical credentials? How much would you be able to prove?

This isn't just a theoretical proposition. After all, would you expect people to buy from you (or invest in your business) based purely on your word? You might claim to pay suppliers a living wage or trade with only environmentally responsible companies, but without solid evidence to back this up, how can other people – including any of your own staff – fully believe in your company? Indeed, if you only have a vague notion of doing something good, how can you truly understand the impact of your business?

When it comes to your finances, there is no such ambiguity. Every pound spent and received needs to be carefully noted in your business's annual accounts. It also allows you and others to assess past successes, and see how well prepared you are for future growth.

Keeping a financial record is compulsory. There is no such legal obligation for your social and environmental impacts. But openness and transparency should be fundamental characteristics of all ethical businesses. If you want to know if you are achieving what you have set out to do – and what that actually means in practice – you will need to find some answers.

Some social impacts might seem impossible to evaluate. It's not easy, for example, to accurately measure the value of creating a company that your staff love to be a part of, or of providing a much-needed service to a disadvantaged community.

But while some things *are* harder to quantify than others, the majority of social and environmental impacts can be properly accounted for. For a small business, this doesn't have to be a heavy burden added to an already hectic schedule. Writing an ethical audit over and above your business accounts might take a little extra time, but there are plenty of associated benefits.

Why bother?

In their book There's No Business Like Social Business, ethical entrepreneurs Liam Black and Jeremy Nicholls give three reasons why accountability and a willingness to be scrutinised independently are the "acid tests" of social business.

1. Better business: The data you gather will actually give a much clearer insight into your business. As a result, you are better positioned to improve your business and enhance the quality of your ethical impacts.

2. Building trust: It can prove your worth to the people who matter to you, and therefore build trust in you and your business. This can increase your chances of winning repeat business and cross-selling.

3. Moral duty: If your enterprise benefits from grant money or financial breaks unavailable to other businesses, there is an obligation to demonstrate what is being achieved by the use of that money.

Business sense

Understanding your social and environmental impacts will help you know whether you are delivering on what you originally set out to do, or not.

Sometimes this seems quite simple: if your ethical aims are simply to buy and sell fair trade goods, you only need to look at your profit and loss account sheet to know how much you've traded. Even so, these figures won't tell you much about the precise impacts of your purchases. If you want to know this, you could find out exactly how much your producers are really being paid and what direct effect your trade is having on their communities.

If you have set up a charitable foundation, and are committed to reducing your waste or pioneering renewable energy, this may be a more difficult task to break down. Perhaps you will understand how well you're doing in one area of the business but have only a vague idea about other elements.

Being able to prove what really makes your business tick is well worth the effort. Besides being a useful way for you to keep track of your social and environmental impacts, ethical accounting has a myriad of other advantages, from motivating your employees through to great PR.

According to AccountAbility, the international professional institute for ethical accounting, it can benefit your business by:

■ Improving your financial performance

■ Enhancing your relationship with stakeholders, e.g. customers, staff

■ Managing risk

■ Managing your relationships with investors

■ Aligning your strategy and operations with your aims and values

■ Establishing your boundaries of responsibility

By creating a record of your social impacts, it will also be easier to explain some of the decisions you make for ethical reasons. If you deliberately recruit employees who need extra care and support, such as people with learning difficulties, you may spend extra time and resources in building up their skills and confidence in a supportive working environment.

AccountAbility
www.accountability21.net

International business membership organisation which aims to increase businesses' adherence to and professionalism in social and ethical accountability.

This may have a negative impact on your balance sheet, but as a non-negotiable, core element of your business, it is one of the costs you are deliberately shouldering. Explaining how you are working to improve people's lives will help to illustrate just why it is a worthwhile pursuit.

Suspicious minds

Proving your social and environmental credentials can also build trust. With record consumer demand for all things ethical, companies are increasingly trying to position themselves as fair and responsible, even when they have very little to show for it. Faced with this PR onslaught, people are increasingly suspicious of anyone who claims to be committed to ethical values.

Trust is also important for your own stakeholders. Depending on your legal structure, you may be reporting to a board of trustees, shareholders or other investors. A properly presented set of ethical accounts will increase their passion for the business.

The right approach

You want to prove your values, but where do you actually start?

The first step in creating an ethical audit is to analyse everything that is important to your business. What are your motivations beyond profit? Who or what are you trying to benefit and what are you doing to achieve this? Your audit has to be accurate and credible, which means you need to consider every part of your business, not just cherry-pick the best bits. These parameters should ideally remain the same, so that you can compare your performances each year.

For start-up businesses, creating this ethical framework should be a relatively simple task.

Whether you're filling in a spreadsheet of charity fundraising targets met and emissions reduced, or applying for ethical kitemarks (see p.199), there are many ways to build up a comprehensive, personal account of your ethical footprint.

Staking the stakeholder

Who is affected by your business? At the most immediate level, this will typically be your employees, suppliers and customers. But on a wider scale, these "stakeholders" may also include your local community, a set of trustees, a partner organisation, perhaps even the whole planet. If you have placed a particularly prominent emphasis on one specific group (social firms, for example, are committed to people with disabilities), they will be an important stakeholder. Once you have thought of everyone who is affected by your business, write them down in order of priority. You can work through them in turn.

If you start up a recruitment business which gives former offenders a helping hand into employment and also offers a percentage of your profits to charities for victims of crime, you will have a number of different stakeholders. These will include the companies you recruit for, the former offenders themselves and their families, your local community (by getting vulnerable people into employment and away from crime), any staff you may employ, the charities you donate to, the victims of crime and their families, society at large (by reducing the number of re-offenders) and the wider economy (by generating employment). Your business will have a measurable effect on all these areas.

Listening

Where you are unsure of any social or environmental impacts, talk to the people who know. If you donate a percentage of profits to charity, for example, find out how the money is being used. If you have implemented a flexible working scheme, ask how that has helped your employees' lives. As well as assessing positive impacts made, this can help you recognise any mistakes or areas for improvement.

There are also ways to measure tangible outputs, such as CO_2 emissions. This not an exact science, but offsetting companies, such as the Climate Neutral Group or Climate Care, will take your business's energy usage and transport activities and produce an instant figure. If you are implementing an energy reduction initiative, comparing annual scores will measure your success.

Verification

Independent verification will give added credibility to any findings. However, as a small business, this may be difficult to arrange in practice. Social accounting experts recommend finding a couple of well-respected people unconnected to the business to read through your report. If this isn't possible, an alternative option is to list all your sources, i.e. the organisations or research that led you to your findings.

If transparency is important to your beliefs, the final results can be sent to stakeholders and published on your website. Putting your social accounts into the public arena also increases understanding of your company's motivations.

On its homepage, the Eden Project in Cornwall evaluates each of its ethical goals, from recycling and waste reduction to supporting its local community:

"By 2006, five years after opening, Eden had – according to independently verified figures – contributed £700 million to the local economy. Eden uses local suppliers wherever possible, employs local people and supports local businesses in Cornwall and the South West."

Seals of approval

The most visible way to prove your ethical credentials is a kitemark. The best-known accreditation scheme in the UK is the **Fairtrade** mark. Guaranteeing preferable payment terms and a living wage to suppliers, it is currently used on more than 1,500 brands nationwide. If you sell or promote Fairtrade certified products, you may be able to use its logo on your website or your promotional materials. The Fairtrade Foundation has a set of usage guidelines, which you need to adhere to; this can be downloaded free from its website.

For all its many benefits, however, Fairtrade accreditation is currently restricted to just 19 core products, and the approval process is limited to examining a company's supply chain. It does not, for example, reveal anything about how a business treats its own staff, or its commitment to the environment.

**Forestry Stewardship
Council**
www.fsc-uk.org

Non-governmental
organisation dedicated
to promoting responsible
management of the
world's forests; awards
certification that wood is
from sustainable sources.

Soil Association
www.soilassociation.org

Campaign organisation
in favour of organic food
and sustainable farming;
also awards organic
certification.

Another problem is that a company, which is otherwise predominantly unethical, can carry one small Fairtrade line and yet still use the kitemark.

Despite these limitations, the success of Fairtrade has paved the way for many other initiatives. Indeed, there are dozens of schemes with different ethical emphases.

Some are industry-specific. If you are running an eco-friendly garden design business or printing company, **Forestry Stewardship Council** accreditation proves that the wood you use does not contribute to the destruction of forests. Depending on your business, other appropriate accreditation labels may include the Marine Stewardship Council, Demeter (for biodynamic food), or Scottish Organic Producers' Association, UKROFS, Ecocert and Organic Food Federation (all organic certification).

In 2006, organic food accreditation body the **Soil Association** created a new, broader ethical logo. Its "ethical trade pilot scheme" covers any organic produce in any country. As well as organic standards, accredited businesses have to demonstrate "fair treatment of workers, a fairer return for farmers and a positive contribution to the local community". This is still a very new stamp, but given the strong public recognition of the Soil Association, it could soon become a must-have accreditation for all organic ethical businesses.

The **Investors in People** (IIP) scheme focuses on your relations with your own employees. By working through a 10-step process, you can understand better how your team is working, and whether your current approach is actually working. The goal is to give everyone in your company the right knowledge, skills and motivation to work efficiently. Not only does this improve staff morale, it also increases company competitiveness and makes it easier to achieve your ethical goals. As a PR tool, the IIP stamp also shows others that your employees' welfare is at the heart of your business.

If you are working with partners in your local community, whether supporting a local school or helping to raise money for a hospital, you can apply for a **CommunityMark** award. A national programme run by independent charity Business in the Community, it rewards businesses which are actively involved in their local community. The process typically takes a month, and you can get advice on writing your application through the CommunityMark network.

The **Ethical Company Organisation** (ECO) runs a much broader accreditation scheme. Businesses are analysed according to 15 specific criteria under three general headings: the environment, animals and people. As part of its award process, ECO checks several thousand documents from NGOs, campaign groups and court reports to see if applicants have been criticised for their behaviour. Accreditation is awarded to companies who score highly (in the top 33 per cent) compared to the other companies in their sector. The research is repeated every 12 months.

If you plan to make ongoing environmental improvements to your business, you could apply for the **Green Mark**. There are three stages to this "environmental excellence" scheme. To win a Level 1 award, you need to prove to an environmental consultant that you have an environmental policy, meet key environmental legislation, have nominated an employee as your company's "environmental champion", and have taken steps to reduce your business's environmental impact. You can win further awards by continuing to show improvements in reducing this environmental impact.

Business in the Community
www.bitc.org.uk

Business-led charity which aims to challenge companies to continually improve the impact they have on society.

Ethical Company Organisation
www.ethical-company-organisation.org

Website enables consumers to easily compare the corporate social responsibility records of hundreds of companies and brands.

The **Rainforest Alliance** is another certification promoting and guaranteeing improvements in agriculture, forestry and travel. The seal ensures goods and services have been produced in compliance with strict guidelines protecting the environment, wildlife and local communities.

Workers' co-operative **Ethiscore** is Ethical Consumer magazine's online shoppers' guide. The magazine runs regular reports on specific products and adds its findings to the website. On average, 30 new products appear every year – from baby bottles to vodka – and manufacturers and retailers are evaluated on the environment, human rights, animal rights, politics and sustainability.

Ethical water company Belu has developed its own accreditation, known as **Penguin**. Carrying the strap-line "Penguin Approved – No Global Warming", the logo will be available to companies committed first to reducing and then offsetting any greenhouse gas emissions. It is being promoted as the first "zero carbon footprint" kitemark for goods and services.

While the majority of ethical stamps will be an asset to your business, you need to be careful about the kind of company you are keeping. The **Ethical Trading Initiative** (ETI), for example, claims "to identify and promote good practice in labour standards in international supply chains". Nevertheless, its corporate membership list includes the likes of Asda (owned by Wal-Mart), Gap and Tesco, some of the most heavily criticised multinationals in the world. While members do have to adhere to certain ETI codes in their operations to get accreditation, critics argue that these companies should not be on any "ethical list".

In 2006, Business in the Community ranked British American Tobacco in its '100 top companies for

Ethical Consumer
www.ethicalconsumer.org

Online information and commercial research service into companies, their ethical practices and standards, as well as a consumer magazine.

corporate responsibility'. Despite the fact that one in two regular smokers will eventually be killed by their habit, it commended the global cigarette manufacturer for "outstanding performance in environmental management and environmental impact".

Richard Reed, co-director of Innocent Drinks, is no stranger to such contradictions: "We got asked to be involved in the launch of (an ethical kitemark) a few years ago," he says, "so I asked them who else was taking part. One was British American Tobacco, another was Ladbrokes. I said, 'Do you honestly think I'm going to sign up to this thing? They sell death and gambling – never mind that they might use recycled paper.'"

A more stringent and transparent ethical kitemark is the **SEE Stamp**. Launched in 2006, it questions applicants on a broad range of social and environmental issues, and also demands that their answers are published in the public domain. This transparency, argues SEE Stamp director Michael Solomon, is essential to any kitemark's credibility.

"We can't allow companies to cherry-pick only the information they want us to see in their CSR reports," he says. "SEE Stamp research shows that 68 per cent of people think companies pretend to be ethical just to sell more products, so we need to be as thorough as possible."

To gain SEE Stamp approval, you need to answer 50 questions, ranging from your employee rights record to environmental impact. The answers are then evaluated, published on its website and open for public comment.

"Going through the process is actually a really interesting experience," says Michael. "The questions can often highlight what you haven't thought of in your business plan, and help you put them in place."

CHECKLIST ✓
Proving it

- ☐ Create a list of stakeholders
- ☐ Record all your environmental and social impacts
- ☐ Seek independent verification
- ☐ Apply for ethical kitemarks
- ☐ Create your own ethical standards

Make your own mark

If there isn't a kitemark for your kind of business, you can always create your own. Jutexpo, an ethical business which makes shopping bags from biodegradable jute, faced just that problem when it began negotiations with Waitrose supermarket. "We'd always had an ethical policy with our suppliers," explains MD Barrie Turner, "but Waitrose insisted on a third-party audit."

With no Fairtrade kitemark for textile production, Barrie had to prove his ethical credentials independently. He arranged for two different auditors to travel to his production site to check on all aspects of Jutexpo's operations, from employee working conditions to environmental impacts. Jutexpo passed the auditors' examination and Waitrose subsequently bought 150,000 wine bags.

The ethical audit didn't only come in useful for that order. The following year, Jutexpo won a tender to supply 25,000 bags to Cheshire County Council. "For us it was a question of credibility," says Richard Bramhall, the council's communications account manager for the environment. "Jutexpo's experience and ethical audit were hugely impressive factors in their favour."

Making the grade

 Want to prove your ethical credentials? Here are five of the 50 questions you need to answer to qualify for the SEE Stamp.

Marketplace ethics

Does your company selectively advertise to vulnerable consumer groups, such as the highly indebted, groups with few market choices or children?

Community

Has your company targeted economically depressed regions for investment?

Workforce

Has your company developed work-life balance options which provide adjustable working patterns whereby employees can combine work with, for example, caring for others or pursuing other aspirations?

Environment

Do your company's environmental policies extend to suppliers and contractors?

Community

Does your company support an employee volunteer scheme for involvement in the local community?

www.seecompanies.com

12 Lift Off

IN THIS CHAPTER...

- ▓ Ethical success stories
- ▓ Innocent Drinks
- ▓ Ecotricity
- ▓ Cafédirect

CONGRATULATIONS. YOU NOW have everything you need to get your ethical business up and running. With a clear understanding of your core beliefs and values, and how you can incorporate them into your everyday decisions, you can get on with making that dream company come to life.

The rewards can be incredible. Whether you're cutting back on your emissions by signing up to a green energy supplier and cycling to work, or choosing to deal only with other socially minded companies, your business will be making a positive difference from day one. Everything counts. Even if you don't share the same vision as bottled water company Belu, who give away 100 per cent of their profits, you will still be effecting a real change.

Paths to success

Smaller, day-to-day decisions can have a huge impact. That's just how organic fashion brand Howies works when it examines every stage of its cotton and denim manufacturing process. From sourcing recycled cotton to rejecting fertilizers and using tougher twine to make its clothes last longer, dozens of tiny decisions help to create a product that is better for its customers and the planet. If you are looking at manufacturing products, Howies is a good role model to follow. Its ethical step-by-step approach has been a massive hit with consumers. In 2005, company turnover tripled to £2.6 million, and it was on course to double that in 2006. All of which is bad news for fertilizer producers and very good news for the organic cotton industry and the environment.

If you want inspiration on how to cut down your energy consumption, take a look at the Eden Project. Perhaps its least innovative green initiative has simply been to switch from disposable to washable cutlery and crockery. Sounds trivial? The decision actually saves nine tonnes of waste from going to landfill every year. A dishwasher has also been installed (creating two permanent jobs in the kitchen) and 700,000 fewer disposable items are now bought each year, greatly reducing transport and energy costs. The Eden Project estimates financial savings of £180,000 over five years. Just from washing up!

Social goals might seem harder to measure, but you can still achieve an incredible amount of change. When Gordon D'Silva set up Training For Life in 1995, he wanted to do something about the debilitating effects of long-term unemployment. If you are thinking about incorporating your ethical values into a wide range of products or services, his experience shows that a broad vision can actually strengthen your impact. Through his entrepreneurial charity, Gordon has helped set up numerous personal development programmes, training courses and back-to-work schemes, as well as several profitable ethical businesses. These include the restaurant Hoxton Apprentice – which provides long-term unemployed people with the skills and training needed to find work in the catering industry – and Met@Lambeth, a community gym. In 2005, Training For Life worked directly with 1,312 people, almost double the number it reached in 2004. Since its launch, the organisation has helped change the lives of more than 8,000 disadvantaged people. This is the kind of impact your business can achieve when you create a network of innovative support and solutions to deal with a particular social issue.

There are hundreds of other inspiring stories of ethical businesses which are growing fast and making an ever greater, longer-lasting difference. Remember, these were all small companies once. Each one had to understand its core values and learn how to work them efficiently into the business, just like you. The following examples are three of the best-known ethical super-brands in the UK. Here's what the people who have taken them to the top consider to be the secret of their success.

Innocent Drinks

In the summer of 1998, three high-flying city workers bought £500 worth of fruit, turned it into smoothies and sold them from a stall at a music festival in London. They posted up a sign, asking 'Do you think

we should give up our jobs to make these smoothies?'
and put out a bin saying "YES" and a bin saying
"NO" At the end of the weekend the "YES" bin was
full. The following day, they resigned. Three months
later, Innocent Drinks was launched.

Eight years of blood, sweat and fruit juice later,
Innocent is one of Britain's most inspirational business
success stories. A runaway market leader in the UK,
it employs more than 100 people and has a projected
2006 turnover of £70 million. Its financial performance
alone is astonishing. But what sets Innocent apart
from many other high-growth businesses is that it
cares about a lot more than just profit.

The company has a bulging ethical portfolio:
Innocent's core product is a healthy, all-natural
drink. As for the day-to-day stuff, supply chains are
checked to guarantee that all partners have strong
social and environmental policies. Closer to home,
the packaging has been continually improved, first
using a 50 per cent recyclable plastic bottle and then
launching a fully recyclable corn starch version. It has
also reduced its CO_2 emissions and offsets the rest.
As an employer, Innocent offers staff share options,
a healthcare plan, a £2,000 bonus on having a baby
and the chance to receive a £1,000 scholarship to
pursue outside interests. Small wonder it has topped
numerous 'Best Company to Work For' surveys. In
2004, it set up the Innocent Foundation. A registered
charity, the foundation invests 10 per cent of all
Innocent's profits into community development
projects in many of the countries from which the
company buys its fruit.

Co-founder Richard Reed doesn't seem surprised
by Innocent's success. As for being a good business,
he says, if the values are there from the start, being

ethical can actually get easier as you grow. "I like the idea that size brings clout. Seven years ago we couldn't get our phone calls returned from our suppliers. When no one even wants to trade with you, can you imagine saying, 'Tell me about the social and environmental practices of your plantation?' That was never going to happen."

Back then, the three founders were still finding their feet. "We were young, we knew nothing about setting up a business, or the sector we were in," says Reed. Worse still, every senior person they managed to get time with had told them they needed to prolong the product's shelf life.

This was a blow to their confidence, but they refused to add preservatives. Being natural was the only thing that set Innocent apart from the competition, so there could be no compromise. Today, Reed says that the best businesses have "a central core that is non-negotiable", but that everything else should be more flexible.

Looking back on the company's success, one of Innocent's key strengths has been finding the right people who share the same set of values. Identifying and resolving weaknesses is a critical part of business survival. Reed sums it up neatly: "You've got to surround yourself with people who are great at the things you're rubbish at."

Having three bosses is unusual for any company. It has occasionally slowed down decision-making, but it has meant they have developed innovative ways to resolve issues. For every new idea, for example, there is a "recommender", who conceives the idea and argues for its implementation, and a "decider", who considers the argument impartially and makes the final decision.

There is another advantage to its management set-up. A company limited by shares, Reed and his two co-founders still own the business outright. Control, he says, is all important, especially when it comes to deciding on ethical policies, such as gifting profits to a charity.

"Me and my two mates run the company so we can do what we like. But if you're a CEO put in charge of a multinational bank, your job is to keep a steady upward share price. If you give away 10 per cent of profits to charity, you're going to get fired because the share price is going to go through the floor. So it is easier for us."

Despite his company's strong social and environmental values, Reed says that he – and any budding ethical entrepreneurs – must remain focused on the business. "I don't expect a single person to buy our smoothies for any other reason than they taste better and are better quality," he says. "The second we think people will buy them because we give 10 per cent of profits to charity or are carbon neutral is a mistake."

Given Innocent's spectacular growth, it's no surprise the company has attracted plenty of interest within the commercial world. Two years ago, a major corporation signalled an interest in buying out the founders. Rather than take the cash, they decided they wanted to "stay in it for the ride", but realised they needed to get bigger quickly. This has been achieved through expansion into other countries, new product lines and more employees.

Growing, Reed insists, is nothing to be afraid of. "Being bigger is better if you know you're getting the right people on board. Our values are now much clearer and people who share those values are attracted to us. The richness is getting greater. I think we're more innocent today than we ever have been."

Ecotricity

Before founding green energy company Ecotricity, Dale Vince spent 10 years living in an army surplus trailer on a hill in Gloucestershire, harnessing wind power for electricity, growing his own food and leading an almost entirely self-sustainable lifestyle. Fast forward to today, and the self-styled eco warrior has helped to bring green energy into the mainstream. Ecotricity now supplies electricity to more than 20,000 customers in the UK, has an annual turnover in excess of £15 million and invests several million pounds in new wind energy projects every year.

"When I started the business, I had £1,000 in all the world... and a welding set," says Dale Vince, reflecting on his very first entrepreneurial venture: building wind turbines. That was in the early 1990s. A passionate environmentalist, Vince had read everything he could about wind energy – still a relatively new concept – in order to power his own makeshift home. Using this knowledge, he won a contract to deliver "shed loads" of wind turbines to Scottish Power.

Despite this big break, Vince felt that mainstream energy companies were largely disinterested in green energy. The commonly held view at the time was that no one wanted it and it would cost too much. "We started up to prove the exact opposite," he says. "We were confident we could deliver green energy for the same price as brown energy."

In 1995, Dale launched the Renewable Energy Company, since renamed Ecotricity. Despite early battles with planning authorities, it has established a firm footing in the UK energy market. It was the first company in the world to offer a green electricity tariff and – despite early cynicism from the mainstream energy industry – its success has undoubtedly helped influence the behaviour of the UK's big six energy companies today.

All six have now entered the green energy market. For Vince, however, this is not unwanted competition – it's something to be encouraged.

"The one thing that will change other energy companies' behaviour is to see us be successful," he says. "Our mission was all about change; we see ourselves as a catalyst."

By 2008, Ecotricity aims to be investing £40 million in new infrastructure for renewable energy. This commitment to building new wind turbines is a key element of its environmental credentials and still sets it apart from the competition. According to the environmental energy watchdog WhichGreen, Ecotricity spent the equivalent of £901.64 per customer on building new renewable energy projects in 2004. Green energy companies Good Energy and Green Energy UK spent nothing at all, instead simply buying up existing green supply. Powergen came second in the league table with an average customer spend of just £9.58.

This deep-rooted commitment to developing future green energy is one reason why Ecotricity's customer base is currently growing by about 2,000 customers a month. In 2007, the company plans to double its wind energy capacity, and to supply power to more than 50,000 households.

Looking back on the company's impressive growth, Vince says that confidence and self-reliance have been crucial to his success: "I took to business like a duck to water. Being a bit of a drop-out can actually make you very self-reliant. You don't take no for an answer. You have to fix your own things. These are all useful skills for an entrepreneur."

He also points to managerial freedom. Being his own boss has meant that key decisions can be made quickly, and never at the cost of the environment: "We have one shareholder, which is me," he says. "So while we have to make profit, we're not about creating dividends. Our mission is altruistic but we have to make money doing it."

Another positive experience has come through co-operation. In recent years, Ecotricity has developed close partnerships with a number of ethical organisations, such as the Soil Association, The Body Shop and Future Forests, all of whom are powered by Ecotricity. In the case of the Soil Association, its members are being encouraged to switch their homes and businesses to Ecotricity. In return, Ecotricity will make a donation to the Soil Association to support the organic movement. It's a win-win situation and something that Vince says more ethical business should be doing.

Perhaps the biggest stepping stone to growth, however, has been securing loan finance. In 2003, Triodos agreed to support a series of new wind turbine projects. To date, the social bank has invested £20 million in Ecotricity, which will be paid back once the turbines are built and generating income. This up-front finance will help the energy company meet its ambitious target of building 500 megawatts of new green energy by 2010.

From a single wind turbine to a multimillion pound enterprise, Vince's eco-company has come a long way in just over 10 years. Does he ever feel it's all getting a bit too big?

"No way," he says. "We're environmentalists doing good business. And we're showing that it can be done. Triodos have put a lot of faith in us, but I'd actually like to stick a nought on the end of that loan.

Building new wind capacity is crucial in the fight against climate change – and there's a lot more work to be done yet."

Cafédirect

When you buy a cup of non-Fairtrade coffee, less than 1 per cent of the retail price typically goes back to the grower. Cafédirect, the first coffee brand in the UK to carry the Fairtrade mark, was set up to give producers a better deal. In 1991, the company began by borrowing three containers of coffee from growers in Mexico, Peru and Costa Rica. Since then, it has grown and developed its own highly successful trading model, which far exceeds the minimum standard for Fairtrade certification. In 2005, it paid £1.6 million to producers above the market price and invested 86 per cent of its operating profits into training programmes in producer countries. It is currently the UK's sixth largest coffee brand and is seventh largest in tea.

When Penny Newman became CEO of Cafédirect in 1998, the ethical hot drinks company employed just four people. The business had always been deeply rooted in fair trade principles, but its products were only starting to appear on supermarket shelves. The brand had yet to become a household name.

"There was a lot of hunger and passion," she recalls, "but we needed to drive the company forward. We had to work hard on our communication and retail."

At the time, fair trade was still a relatively unknown concept. Besides educating people about its social goals, Cafédirect was also trying to understand and exploit a new and growing market. At the time, it was selling four different products – just one tenth of its current product line.

Penny, who brought retail and marketing experience from her previous position at The Body Shop, was looking for a sharp increase in sales. "Within six months of joining, I did a business plan and thought if we put our minds to it, the company could really go places. But we needed people and money."

She began by building a "virtual company" to complement the existing skills gaps. It is a policy that continues to this day. As the UK's largest Fairtrade coffee brand, Cafédirect might easily be perceived as being as large as its multinational competitors, but it still only employs 30 people.

"I've always felt you can look outside your business and bring people in when you need them," says Penny. "We have now developed about 50 different partnerships with other organisations – from marketing and selling, to manufacturing. This 'virtual company' helps us to say flexible and nimble, and focused on what we do best."

As the Fairtrade movement caught on among consumers, Cafédirect began growing by around 20 per cent every year. Penny identified a clear opportunity to turn what had been a niche brand into one of the world's biggest coffee buyers. The problem was how to raise sufficient capital for the growth without compromising the company's core values.

Cafédirect had originally been created by Oxfam and three fair trade ventures, Traidcraft, Equal Exchange and Twin Trading. At one point, the board of directors considered inviting in a fifth shareholder. But then they realised there was another way to increase investment, which would bring fair trade principles into their management structure too.

In 2004, the board was expanded to include two

representatives: one from a coffee co-operative and one from tea partners, with whom the company have long-term partnerships. This was achieved alongside a public share issue, which raised £5 million and, for the first time, saw growers and customers take a share of the business. To safeguard Cafédirect's core values, no one investor can own more than 15 per cent of the shares.

This capital has enabled the business to capitalise on the boom in demand for fairly traded drinks. Since the share issue, turnover has risen by 14 per cent to nearly £20 million. Today, the company works with 37 producer organisations across 12 different countries and is ranked third most trusted household brand for social responsibility.

For the growers, this means more business and better wages, as well as increased investment in their communities. In 2005, for example, Cafédirect spent £574,000 on business and technical training programmes for its producers.

For Penny, Cafédirect's incredible success is something of a self-fulfilling prophecy:

"You have to think big," she explains. "If you have that mindset, then doors will open for you. Growing a business is not always easy, but it's worthwhile if you are comfortable with that kind of challenge. For us, it's simple: the more sales we make, the more positive impact we can make. That's why we want to be as big as possible."

Index

Where Next?

THROUGHOUT THE BOOK, we've highlighted dozens of useful ethical support services and specialist green companies. Now you are ready to turn your business idea into reality, you may need to call on these and other professional organisations: from legal eagles and marketing mentors to eco suppliers and ethical magazines.

To get you on your way, we've compiled a starter directory of handy resources. We hope this will help set your ethical business on course for success.

RESOURCES GUIDE

Raising Finance

Adventure Capital Fund
Government funding and support scheme, which invests in local communities by helping organisations be more sustainable.
020 7488 3455 / info@adventurecapitalfund.org.uk
www.adventurecapitalfund.org.uk

Ashoka
Global association of the world's leading social entrepreneurs, runs a venture fund for outstanding social entrepreneurs.
020 7961 6506 / infoUK@ashoka.org
www.ashoka.org

BIGinvest
A Big Issue magazine funding initiative, which helps finance social enterprises.
020 7074 0060 / enquiries@biginvest.co.uk
www.biginvest.co.uk

Bridges Community Ventures
An innovative venture capital company which invests in ambitious businesses located in the most economically disadvantaged parts of England.
020 7262 5566 / info@bridgesventures.com
www.bridgesventures.com

British Bankers Association
Trade association for banks whose website gives a very useful summary of the different types of social enterprise, and financial and banking support currently available.
www.bba.org.uk

Business Gateway
Scottish Executive partnership, which offers information, funding and support to start-up businesses in Scotland.
0845 609 6611
www.bgateway.com

Calouste Gulbenkian Foundation
Grant-giving organisation which funds various local community groups that work, for example, towards financial inclusion, environmental awareness and benefiting older people.
020 7636 5313 / info@gulbenkian.org.uk
www.gulbenkian.org.uk

CEFET
Consultancy company which helps third sector organisations access European funding.
0115 911 0419 / info@cefet.org.uk
www.cefet.org.uk

Charity Bank
The world's first not-for-profit bank, set up by Charities Aid Foundation. It lends some £18 million to charities and social enterprises in the UK.
01732 774040 / enquiries@charitybank.org
www.charitybank.org

Community Accountancy Network
A network of organisations which offer training, advice and information in financial management to local voluntary and third sector organisations.
0115 947 0839 / caplus@communityaccounting.co.uk
www.communityaccountancy.freeserve.co.uk

Community Development Finance Association
A trade association for independent financial institutions which provide capital and support to sustainable organisations in disadvantaged communities.
020 7430 0222 / info@cdfa.org.uk
www.cdfa.org.uk

Co-operative Bank
The biggest high-street, ethical bank, with downloads of its annual Ethical Consumerism Report, a useful resource for your research and business plan.
08457 212 212 / customerservice@co-operativebank.co.uk
www.co-operativebank.co.uk

Esmée Fairbairn Foundation
One of the largest independent grant making organisations in the UK, which funds projects that aim to improve the quality of life for people and communities.
020 7297 4700 / info@esmeefairbairn.org.uk
www.esmeefairbairn.org.uk

European Union Social Fund (EUSF)
One of four Structural Funds designed to strengthen economic and social cohesion in the European Union, which has been one of the largest grant providers to UK businesses.
esf.feedback@dfes.gsi.gov.uk
www.esf.gov.uk

Foursome
London-based equity company which offers early-stage investment opportunities for "innovative growth businesses seeking to create a positive social and environmental impact – as well as achieve significant financial returns".
020 7833 0555 / mail@foursome.net
www.foursome.net

Futurebuilders
A government-backed £125 million investment fund, which provides a combination of loans, grants and support for organisations that deliver public services.
0191 261 5200 / info@futurebuilders-england.org.uk
www.futurebuilders-england.org.uk

Government Funding Portal
Online resource run by the charity Directory of Social Change which allows you to search for what government grants your business might be eligible for.
020 7391 4800 / enquiries@dsc.org.uk
www.governmentfunding.org.uk

Industrial Common Ownership Finance
Initiative which has been providing loan finance for co-operatives, employee owned businesses and social enterprises for 30 years.
01179 166750 / info@co-opandcommunityfinance.coop
www.icof.co.uk

Finance to start up and grow your social enterprise

london **rebuilding** society

Whatever your type of organisation, London Rebuilding Society has a financial product that meets your needs

We offer business loans up to £250,000 at competitive rates

But if you're not quite ready to borrow, our smartfinance package of business coaching, training and workshops will get you up to speed

And because our approach is hands-on, we have brought our training services in-house in new premises with purpose-built, disabled-access facilities

Our training and meeting rooms are also available for hire

Everything you want under one roof

London Rebuilding Society
9 Bonhill Street London EC2A 4PE
T: 020 7682 1666 F: 020 7682 1417
E: info@londonrebuilding.com W: www.londonrebuilding.com

Local Investment Fund
Government-led scheme that has eight regional funds and provides finance for community enterprises involved in regeneration in England.
020 7680 1028 / information@lif.org.uk
www.lif.org.uk

London Rebuilding Society
An independent funding organisation, which lends re-payable loans to businesses that create jobs and opportunities supporting local communities.
020 7682 1666 / info@londonrebuilding.com
www.londonrebuilding.com

New Entrepreneur Scholarship Programme
Government initiative which offers funding and support to people living in disadvantaged areas to start in business.
020 7300 7252 / nesadmin@nfea.com
www.nesprogramme.org

Regional Development Agencies
A network of organisations which report to the government and support regional economic development and regeneration around the UK.
www.englandsrdas.com

"One person's evil multinational is another job-seeker's munificent contributor to the community. The Ethical Careers Guide can steer you through the complexities."
Lucy Siegle, The Observer

THE ETHICAL CAREERS GUIDE is the essential careers handbook for everyone who wants to make the world a better place.

www.ethicalcareers.org

Smile
Online sister to the ethical Co-operative Bank.
0870 843 2265 / questions_for_you@smile.co.uk
www.smile.co.uk

The Big Lottery Fund
Hands out about £630 million of lottery money annually to various sustainable business projects.
0845 4102030 / general.enquiries@biglotteryfund.org.uk
www.biglotteryfund.org.uk

The Department of Trade and Industry
A government department responsible for trade and business and a handy source of information for many grants.
020 7215 5000 / dti.enquiries@dti.gsi.gov.uk
www.dti.gov.uk

The Ecology Building Society
Building society which loans money to projects which have a beneficial impact on the environment, including "small scale ecological businesses".
0845 674 5566 / info@ecology.co.uk
www.ecology.co.uk

The Small Firms Loan Guarantee Scheme
A Department of Trade and Industry initiative which is aimed at start-ups and young businesses who find it difficult to raise enough finance.
020 7215 5000 / dti.enquiries@dti.gsi.gov.uk
www.dti.gov.uk

Triodos Bank
Ethical bank which uses investors' money to finance companies, institutions and projects that add "cultural value" and benefit people and the environment.
0117 973 9339 / mail@triodos.co.uk
www.triodos.co.uk

Unity Trust Bank
Socially responsible bank which specialises in providing membership and banking services to trade union, charity, voluntary, credit union, and membership organisation sectors.
0845 140 1000 / utb@unity.co.uk
www.unitygroup.co.uk

UnLtd
A charity that has two tiers of grant-giving aimed at "people with vision, drive, commitment and passion who want to change the world for the better".
0845 850 1122 / info@unltd.org.uk
www.unltd.org.uk

Business & IP Centre

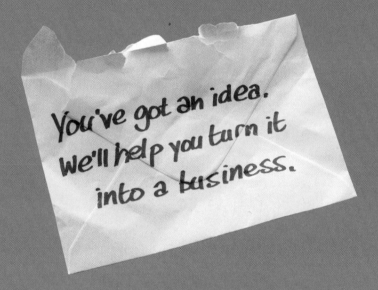

All the facts, figures and guidance you need to get your business idea off to a good start. Free, at the British Library, Euston Road. ⊖⇄ King's Cross or Euston. For information on how to join, go to **www.bl.uk/bipc**

Our name is our conscience

The Open University is open to people, open to places, open to methods and open to ideas.

We promote educational opportunity and social justice by providing high-quality personal and professional development to all who wish to realise their ambitions and fulfil their potential.

For more information contact us on + 44 (0)1908 655767 or visit www.open.ac.uk/employers

Venturesome risk investment fund

Run by the Charities Aid Foundation, this fund aims to finance charity ventures deemed high risk by the Community Development Financial Institutions.
020 7832 3056
www.cafonline.org

Access Funds

Useful site that points to NGO and third sector funding sources such as central government, the National Lottery, devolved governing bodies, EU and quangos.
020 7871 5237 / info@access-funds.co.uk
www.access-funds.co.uk

j4b

An online resource into which you can enter all your business details and find out what government grants your business can apply for.
01625 628 007 / j.phillips@j4b.com
www.j4b.co.uk

... comm..
.isibility sustainabil..
.imunity ethics environm.
.y globalisation business cor
.nt corporate responsibility sus
.ion business community ethics
responsibility sustainability glol
community ethics environment **MSc in**
y ethics environment corporat
ty globalisation businessResponsibility &
corporate responsibility
'siness communityBusiness Practice
'litv sustain-

Challenging the way you think and act

As social, environmental and ethical issues, such as climate change, world poverty, and energy futures have moved up the public agenda, the question of 'responsibility' in the context of business practice is now a major topic for debate. The MSc in Responsibility and Business Practice is an innovative two-year part-time management degree which explores the complex relationships involved and helps participants develop their working practice in this field.

If you are concerned about corporate responsibility, sustainability, social justice and the role of business in society, this could be the course for you.

www.bath.ac.uk/management
E. mscrbp@management.bath.ac.uk
T. +44 (0) 1225 383861

EQUIS
EFMD
ACCREDITED
UNIVERSITY OF
BATH
SCHOOL OF MANAGEMENT

Going Green

Calverts

London-based ethical printers which has worked hard to minimize its environmental impact.
020 7739 1474 / info@calverts.coop
www.calverts.coop

Can do Exchange

An online forum aimed at community organisations which allows them to share ideas, skills, contacts and resources.
0870 4207976 / info@candoexchange.org
www.candoexchange.org

Carbon balancing

Run by international conservation charity the World Land Trust, this website allows organisations to calculate their carbon output and the best way of off-setting it.
0845 054 4422 / info@worldlandtrust.org
www.carbonbalanced.org

Climate Care

Commercial "offsetting" company, which your company can pay to account for and offset your carbon emissions by planting trees and supporting environment projects.
01865 207 000 / mail@climatecare.org
www.climatecare.org

Community Broadband Network

Organisation which helps community projects set up and access affordable broadband connections.
0845 456 2466
www.broadband-uk.coop

Ecotricity

Electricity supplier which invests customers' money in funding renewable energy sources.
01453 756 111 / info@ecotricity.co.uk
www.ecotricity.co.uk

Energy Saving Trust

Government funded organisation promoting sustainable use of energy which can provide information on Department of Trade and Industry grants for installing solar energy generating equipment.
020 7222 0101
www.est.org.uk

Envirowise
Offers UK businesses free, independent advice and support on practical ways to increase profits, minimise waste and reduce environmental impact.
0800 585794
www.envirowise.gov.uk

Ethical Property Company
An investment group which buys and develops buildings for ethical businesses.
0845 458 3853 / mail@ethicalproperty.co.uk
www.ethicalproperty.co.uk

Greening the Office
A Friends of the Earth Scotland online resource which offers a web audit so you can see how "green" your office is by assessing everything from what recycling your company does to which energy supplier you use.
0131 554 9977
www.green-office.org.uk

Green Tomato Cars
London-based private hire taxi firm which uses "green cars" and plants trees to help minimize its impact on the environment.
020 8748 8881 / mail@greentomatocars.com
www.greentomatocars.com

Green Your Office
A one-stop online shop for sourcing ethical office supplies and cleaning services.
0845 456 4540 / info@greenyouroffice.co.uk
www.greenyouroffice.co.uk

Liftshare
Car sharing and transport information service which allows you to match your own or your employees' car journeys online with others doing the same route.
08700 780225 / info@liftshare.com
www.liftshare.org

NetRegs
A government website which aims to help small businesses comply with environmental legislation.
08708 506 506 / enquiries@environment-agency.gov.uk
www.netregs.gov.uk

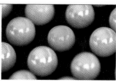
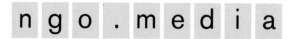

Recycle More

Online information and guidance centre for all aspects of recycling in the workplace, as well as advice on future environmental legislation.
08450 682 572 / info@valpak.co.uk
www.recycle-more.co.uk

The Carbon Trust

Free, practical help and advice on saving money by reducing energy use, and to help accelerate innovative low-carbon technologies.
0800 085 2005 / customercentre@carbontrust.co.uk
www.carbontrust.co.uk

Waste Resource Action Programme

Not-for-profit company which helps businesses to reduce waste, use more recycled material and recycle more things more often.
01295 819 900 / info@wrap.org.uk
www.wrap.org.uk

Business Support

Association of Charitable Foundations

Non-governmental organisation which provides UK-wide support including financial and training for grant-making trusts and foundations of all types.
020 7255 4499 / acf@acf.org.uk
www.acf.org.uk

British Chamber of Commerce

Claims to be the voice of British business and hosts lots of useful resources and directories for business start-ups.
020 7654 5800 / info@britishchambers.org.uk
www.chamberonline.co.uk

Business Balls

Free online resources, forms and tools for the ethical development of people, business and organisations.
0116 235 5585 / ac@alanchapman.com
www.businessballs.com

Business Boffins

A business mentoring service which has a service called "Communities in Business" that is specifically aimed at social enterprises.
01844 278448 / info@businessboffins.com
www.businessboffins.com

Business Link

Government's business support network, with downloadable resources, online advice, local offices and lots of free help available.
0845 600 9 006
www.businesslink.gov.uk

Buyethic

An online prospectus which offers social enterprises the opportunity to find out about tender opportunities within the public sector.
0131 539 8051 / stephanie.wilson@forthsector.org.uk.
www.buyethic.com

Charity Commission

Regulator for charities in England and Wales, deals with registration of new charities and foundations, provides advice and support.
0845 300 0218
www.charity-commission.gov.uk

Community Action Network

Support and networking organisation set up by three social entrepreneurs to help other ethical enterprises transform deprived communities.
0845 456 2537 / canhq@can-online.org.uk
www.can-online.org.uk

Community Enterprise Wales

Largest network of community enterprises in Wales which offers members information on training, funding and grants.
01495 356734 / admin@cewales.co.uk
www.communityenterprisewales.com

Companies House

Government's register of companies, with downloadable information and searchable database.
0870 33 33 636 / enquiries@companies-house.gov.uk
www.companieshouse.gov.uk

Enterprise4All

A not for profit company which helps support new and established minority ethnic businesses to start, grow and succeed.
0845 607 0786 / info@enterprise4all.co.uk
www.enterprise4all.co.uk

Ethical Consumer Research Association
Online information and commercial research service on companies, their ethical practices and standards, as well as a consumer magazine.
0161 226 2929 / mail@ethicalconsumer.org
www.ethicalconsumer.org

Ethical Junction
Very thorough online database of ethically motivated companies, in all sorts of fields and industries.
023 80016224 / membership@ethical-junction.org
www.ethical-junction.org

National Federation of Enterprise Agencies
Website which allows you to find your local Enterprise Agency and also offers a free, confidential business advice service.
01234 831623 / enquiries@nfea.com
www.nfea.com

Payroll Giving Centre
Information centre about payroll giving aimed at businesses, charities and the general public, with guidance materials, resources and downloads.
0845 602 6786 / info@payrollgivingcentre.org.uk
www.payrollgivingcentre.org.uk

Pilotlight
Recruits experienced managers and experts from the private sector to work as volunteers with charities, to share their expertise.
020 7396 7414 / pilotlight@pilotlight.org.uk
www.pilotlight.org.uk

Prime
Not for profit company, a subsidiary of charity Age Concern, which offers advice, information and support to the over 50s who want to start up new businesses.
020 8765 7833 / prime@ace.org.uk
www.primeinitiative.org.uk

P3 Capital
A consultancy firm that provides a range of strategic advisory services to dynamic, high-growth businesses whose products and services create social and environmental value.
08453 455288 / info@p3capital.com
www.p3capital.com

Red Ochre
London-based business consultancy which specialises in advising ethical businesses.
020 7785 6295 / info@redochre.org.uk
www.redochre.org.uk

Social Enterprise Training And Support (SETAS)

Offers consultancy, training, advice and resources specifically about starting and growing a social enterprise.
l.cowell@coin-street.org
www.setas.co.uk

Start Ups

Comprehensive and free information for starting your own business.
020 8334 1608 / oliverm@crimsonbusiness.co.uk
www.startups.co.uk

Striding Out

Business support network for young people, aged 18-30, with enterprising ambitions, offering training, networking, coaching and events.
020 7841 8950 / info@stridingout.co.uk
www.stridingout.co.uk

2amase

A consultancy company which offers advice, training and information for new and existing social enterprises, social entrepreneurs, voluntary and community organisations.
020 8460 1170 / info@2amase.org.uk
www.2amase.org.uk

Structures and Legal

Community Interest Companies Regulator

Government organisation, which registers businesses as CICs if they meet certain community benefiting criteria.
029 20346228 / cicregulator@companieshouse.gov.uk
www.cicregulator.gov.uk

Co-operatives UK

Umbrella body and forum, which provides legal advice for, raises awareness of, and provides a voice for, large and small co-operative enterprises.
0161 246 2900 / info@cooperatives-uk.coop
www.cooperatives-uk.coop

Employee Ownership Options

Organisation set up by the EU to provides advice and guidance on setting up employee-owned business.
0845 603 9197
www.employee-ownership.org.uk

Governance Hub

Offers a set of principles for charities and voluntary organisations which explain the roles of the board of trustees to ensure high standards of governance.
020 7520 2514 / governance.hub@ncvo-vol.org.uk
www.governancehub.org.uk

LawWorks

An independent charity which has over 50 law firms who have agreed to provide free legal advice to small charities, voluntary and community organisations and social enterprises in England and Wales.
020 7929 5601
www.lawworks.org.uk

Social Enterprise Coalition

Umbrella body for member organisations in the social enterprise sector, which supports and represents their work, influences national policy and promotes best practice.
020 7793 2326 / officemanager@socialenterprise.org.uk
www.socialenterprise.org.uk